DATE DUE			
Mar 16 78			
Jan 20 7 9			
Apr 3 7 9			
Feb 22 '83			
Mar 9 8 4			
Dec 26 84			
No 10 1989			
AG 10 1992			
SE 18 1993			

Kids' CLOTHES

by Meredith Gladstone

A Sewing Book

BY MEREDITH & GARY GLADSTONE

Kids' CLOTHES

by Meredith Gladstone

William Morrow and Company, Inc. New York

Books by the Gladstones

The Needlepoint Alphabet Book
Kids' Clothes by Meredith Gladstone

Printed in the United States of America.

1 2 3 4 5   80 79 78 77 76

DESIGNED BY SALLIE BALDWIN/CRAVEN & EVENS, CREATIVE GRAPHICS

Library of Congress Cataloging in Publication Data

Gladstone, Meredith.
    Kids' clothes by Meredith Gladstone.

    1. Children's clothing.   I. Gladstone, Gary, joint author.
II. Title.
TT635.G55   646'.36   75-28402
ISBN 0-688-02994-9

Contents

Introduction

Children are very special people, we all agree. Each child is unique, and each child's clothes should be as special as he is! At the same time, because children sparkle naturally, I don't feel they need to wear clothes that are gimmicky or overdesigned; they look best in simple, uncomplicated dresses and trousers. For this book, I have designed four basic patterns for both boys and girls ages 1 to 5 that are simple to make, easy to wear, fun to decorate, and practical.

All of the sewing techniques are easy, and my husband Gary's photos will help take any mystery out of the instructions. Each pattern has many variations, so you can make one pattern serve several purposes, or you can combine patterns to make a whole wardrobe for your child. Using different fabrics and altering the patterns slightly, you can make clothes for every season and every occasion. From the jacket pattern alone, you can make the jacket, a coat, a bathrobe, a painting smock, a pinafore, or even a big roomy play shirt. The overalls made in corduroy with a turtleneck sweater are perfect for play on a cool day, while the same overalls, cut short in denim, would be cool and comfortable on a hot summer day.

It's important that children's clothes be practical. Sewing them yourself is the first step toward beating the budget; the only real expense is the fabric, and that should be minimal. Throughout the book, I've also suggested ways I've found to make the clothes themselves more durable and long-lasting. Seams and hems can be reinforced in many different ways so that a garment can take repeated washings and lots of activity. Deep hem allowances and adjustable buttons and straps permit the clothes to grow with the child. My 3-year-old son Gregory is at a point where he is growing tall quickly, but his clothing size is not changing. I cut his pants with extra-long legs, cuff them, then turn them down as he grows. This way, his clothes last much longer.

Decorating the clothes you make can be the most fun of all. Many of my favorite patterns for appliqué, patchwork, monograms, embroidery, and pockets are included, ready for you to trace right out of the book. These ideas have been inspired from a variety of sources: American folk art, modern and ancient art, and even advertising graphics. Design ideas abound everywhere, so once you have mastered the basic decorating techniques, try creating your own designs. Museums, art books, and even your local fabric store can serve as stimulating idea mills for your projects. Don't overlook greeting cards or gift wrappings for design motifs to copy or interpret for your own use.

These decorating techniques need not be used only on the clothes in this book. If you don't want to make an entire garment, use any of these ideas on store-bought clothes or on clothes you already have. Patti, a friend of ours, bought Gregory a pair of overalls and made them special for him by decorating them with embroidered "G's." You can also use the patterns to decorate clothes for other members of the family besides just the kids. Gary now has a chambray work shirt monogrammed with the multicolored embroidered "G" pattern and decorated all around the pockets. Pamper yourself, too! It's great fun knowing that no one in the whole world has a shirt exactly like yours.

We hope that you'll enjoy sewing and decorating these clothes. Do try creating a whole wardrobe for your child that is uniquely yours and uniquely his. And most of all, have fun!

Basic Sewing Instructions

Basic Sewing Instructions

THE BASIC PATTERNS

For this book, I've designed four basic sewing patterns: a button shoulder dress, a button shoulder jumpsuit (which girls can wear as well as boys!), a bibbed overall or jumper (which can be worn without the bib as a plain pants or a skirt), and a jacket that can also be a smock or tunic. Generally the patterns fit children 1 to 5 years old, and with minor alterations can fit bigger or smaller children.

I've also included two basic sweater patterns as well as directions for a hat. The first sweater is made with a flat stockinette stitch. It has raglan sleeves, and can be made in a solid color or in stripes, with or without a turtleneck. The other is a fisherman's knit sweater that is a little heavier —perfect for cool days in place of a jacket. Both sweaters are ideal to wear under or with the sewn clothes. Try coordinating your knitting yarns with your fabrics to create exciting, fun effects.

Each basic pattern can have many variations. Depending on the fabric and decorations you use, it can be sporty for play or dressy for special occasions. Garments can be cut long or short, decorated with appliqué, embroidery, or pockets or made of virtually any fabric. Anything goes when you are the designer.

With each pattern, I have given a sketch page of suggestions to inspire you. Try your own sketch pages. Simply trace the basic sketch of the pattern you want to make and fill in with your own motif. Change the style by adding a zipper, a pocket, or anything else you might want to try. Make as many tracings as you wish and try lots of different things. Don't be afraid to make mistakes. It's the best way to learn and find out what you really want to make. Play with fabric swatches of different patterns and colors, experimenting with different combinations. Have fun with the projects and think about the clothes in terms of paper dolls. Design a whole wardrobe on paper and then

SELECTING FABRICS

Although fabric costs rise continually, it is still more economical to make clothes than to buy them ready-made. I love to sew, and enjoy designing because I have my own ideas about what kinds of clothes look best on children. I rarely find children's clothes I like, and if I do, they cost a fortune. I can make them for less than half the retail price, in fact some things would be impossible to produce commercially. Quite often, you can even pick up remnants of fabrics that are perfect for children's clothes because not much yardage is required. Scraps of fabrics you might already have from other projects are ideal for trim, facings, or appliqué.

Today, you can choose from many different types of fabrics, and the fabric you choose will determine the look of the garment. Denim, for example, suggests a sporty active outfit and will take a lot of rough treatment. Velveteen, on the

Jacket

Button shoulder dress with bloomers

Button shoulder jumpsuit

Overalls with variations

other hand, suggests a dressier outfit because the fabric itself is more fragile. Using the same basic pattern, a garment in denim will look totally different from one made in velveteen. The decoration you choose to put on it will also influence the final look. Consider how you want your finished garment to be used when selecting your fabric.

Most children are tough on clothes so I prefer fabrics that can withstand a child's abuse and still look good. Woven cotton blends (that is, blends of cotton and synthetic fibers) are the most practical. These include woven blends of denim, poplin, duck, corduroy, and gabardine, to mention a few. They are easy to work with, can be thrown in the washing machine and dryer, and need little or no ironing. All cotton is ideal too, though it tends to wrinkle more than a blended fabric.

You can also use knits, but keep in mind they are difficult to embroider or appliqué because they have a tendency to stretch. The seams in knitted garments also require special attention. A straight machine stitch does not stretch when pulled, but a knit fabric does, which causes the stitches to break. Some of the newer machines have special stretch stitches for knits. If you are using a straight stitch machine, the fabric must be stretched while you are sewing the seam.

Wool flannels, velveteen, and other less carefree fabrics work beautifully. They can not endure the wear and tear that the washable blends can, but look and tailor so well they are worth using. Any fabric can be washed by hand using cold water and Woolite. I've used these fabrics for clothes for Gregory because I love them; I just don't use them for his play clothes.

You might also consider creating your own patchwork fabric by sewing together different pieces of fabrics, patterns, or colors. I save outgrown jeans, cut them up into flat pieces, and sew them together again. Scraps of fabrics left over from other projects are also useful. The patches can be odd shapes or all uniform squares. Make each piece of patchwork large enough to cut out each piece of your pattern.

Whatever fabric you choose, make sure you check contents for cleaning instructions. If there is any question about colorfastness or shrinkage in a fabric, wash or steam press the fabric *before* you cut out the garment. With a washable fabric, throw it in a hot wash, dry it, press, and then cut out the garment. For wool and other unwashable fabrics, press the entire piece of fabric using a pressing cloth and steam iron. A clean linen dishtowel or a piece of cotton muslin makes a good pressing cloth. Wet the cloth and wring it out so that it is damp but not dripping. Place it on the fabric and press. When the cloth is dry, re-wet it and continue steam pressing until the entire piece is finished. Now you can lay out the pattern and cut the garment out. Use the pressing cloth on the seams too if you think an iron might leave an impression or stain on the fabric.

Patchwork denim made of scraps from old jeans.

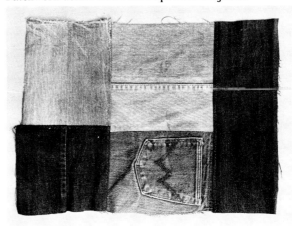

Patchwork fabric made of scraps from other projects.

13

SEWING SUPPLIES

Below is a list of essential tools and materials needed for sewing.

1. *A yardstick* and *a right angle, 2″-wide see-through ruler:* These tools are needed for drawing lines accurately when copying patterns.

2. *Large paper:* A roll of wrapping paper works well for making patterns. Paper printed with 1″ squares is available in some fabric stores.

3. *Marking tools:*
   a. Pens or pencils for making paper patterns
   b. Chalk, tailor's crayon, or pencil, available in any sewing supply store, for marking fabrics

4. *Straight dressmaker pins*

5. *Tape measure* and *a 6″ ruler:* To use for measuring seams at the sewing machine

6. *Scissors:* 8″ shears are best for cutting out the garment in fabric. A small pair, 2″ or 4″, are good for trimming. Pinking shears are useful for trimming seams.

7. *A sewing machine*

8. *A steam iron* and *an ironing board*

FINDING THE CORRECT PATTERN SIZE

	SMALL	MEDIUM	LARGE
	1–2	3–4	5–6
Chest	20″	22″	24″
Waist	19½″	20½″	21½″
Approximate Height	31″	38″	43″

These measurements correspond with the three sizes of each pattern, small, medium, and large. The basic pattern is slightly larger than these measurements because ease is built into each piece. To find out what size a child should wear, measure his chest, waist, and height. Look at the measurement chart and pick the size closest to the child's measurements. Since none of the garments fit skin-tight, the measurements do not need to match exactly. Chest and waist measurements are the most important since the length can be changed easily. Make and cut out the pattern in paper and hold it up to the child to get a rough idea as to how it will look. Make alterations on the paper pattern and then cut it out of fabric.

HOW TO COPY THE PATTERNS

Each pattern in this book is printed on ¼″ graph. This means that 1 square on the graph pattern is equal to 1 square inch on your final pattern. There are 3 sizes graded on each pattern (small, medium, large) so work only with the size you wish to use. The pattern as graphed does not have seam or hem allowances. Once you have copied the pattern, add allowances of ½″ to ¾″ for seams and as deep a hem as you wish.

1. To prepare your pattern paper, calculate the longest and widest point of each pattern piece by counting the squares on the graph. Add 4″ to 7″ in length and 1″ to 2″ to the width for hem and seams. For example: A dress front may be 9″ long (9 squares long) by 8″ wide. Add 4″ to the length (13″) and 1″ to the width (9″) and cut a piece of paper 9″ by 13″.

2. On the paper draw horizontal and vertical lines 1″ apart to form a 1″ graph. A 2″ plastic see-through ruler works best for this.

3. Draw in freehand the lines of the pattern piece you wish to copy, using the squares as your guide lines. Duplicate the part of a line that appears on the ¼″ graph square to the corresponding square on the 1″ graph. (Don't be frightened; this is very simple.)

4. Draw all the pattern pieces before you cut them out. Label each piece as you draw it so that you don't confuse the pieces.

5. Make any alterations on your paper pattern. If you have doubts about fit, cut the paper pattern out and hold it up to the child.

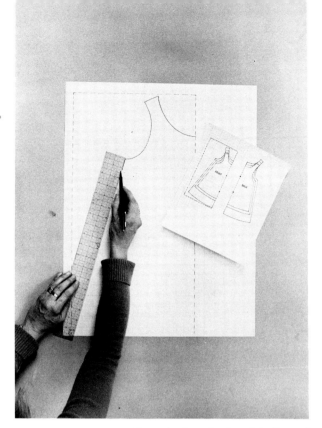

To copy a pattern on a 1″ graph, draw freehand the lines of the pattern piece you wish to copy, using the corresponding squares on the ¼″ graph as your guide.

ADJUSTMENTS AND ALTERATIONS

1. To *alter the length* of any of the basic garments, find a point about ⅓ up from the bottom of the pattern and draw a horizontal line. The line should be perpendicular to the straight grain line. To shorten, fold away excess along drawn line and re-draw side seams. To lengthen, cut the pattern along the horizontal line adding as much paper between the pieces as you need to achieve the extra length and connect the side seams.

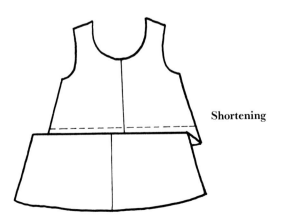

Shortening

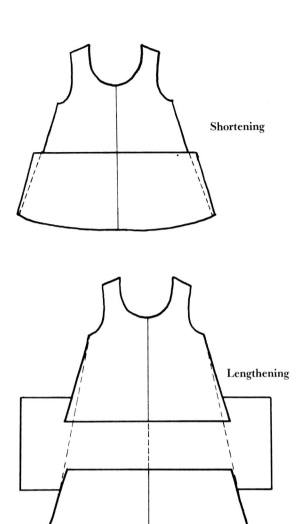

Shortening

Lengthening

2. To *shorten or lengthen a crotch seam* draw a horizontal line on the pattern about ⅓ up from the bottom of the crotch making the line perpendicular to the straight grain line. Lengthen or shorten at this point the same way you would alter length. (See above.)

3. To leave room for growing, I often make pants with *cuffs* so they can eventually be turned down. To allow for a cuff, add twice the width of the cuff you want plus 1″ to the bottom of the pant leg. For instance, if you want a 1½″ cuff, add 4″ to the bottom.

4. By moving *buttons* on shoulders and on straps you can lengthen or shorten a garment. I have allowed for this on the patterns. If you want still more allowance, cut straps longer or extend the back strap on the button shoulder garments.

5. *Hems* can also be let down as children grow, so I suggest you allow at least 3″ turnback.

15

SEAM ALLOWANCES

Allow ½″ to ¾″ for seams and 2″ to 4″ for hems. If you are sure the pattern fits well, ½″ is enough for seams, but if you want more fabric for allowances, cut ¾″ seams. Make sure your seam allowance is the same width around the entire pattern because you will use that measurement as a guide when you are sewing the garment together.

Seam allowances can be added to either the paper pattern or the fabric. If you choose to add the seam allowances on the fabric, make sure you leave enough room all around the pattern when placing it on the fabric.

GRAIN LINES

Grain lines are the direction the threads run in woven fabric. The *straight grain* is an imaginary line that runs parallel to the selvage or length of the fabric. The *cross grain* is the imaginary line

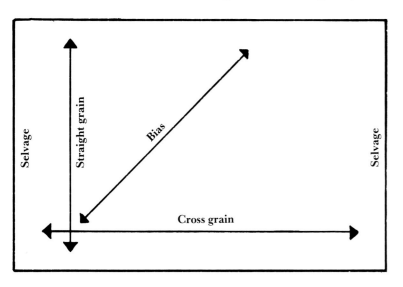

running at right angles to the straight grain or the direction of threads across the fabric. The straight grain should run vertically in a finished garment so that it hangs and wears well. Each pattern piece has the straight grain line noted with a double pointed arrow. The pattern grain line and fabric should be matched up before cutting.

16

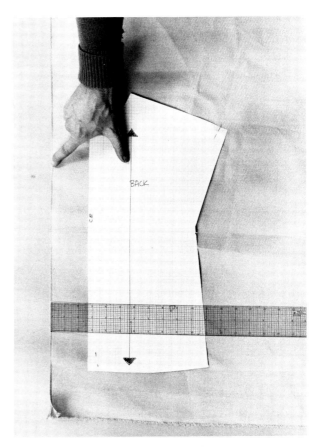

To find the straight grain, line up the grain line marked on each pattern piece with the selvage of the fabric. Make sure the measurement is the same all along the grain line.

To do this line up straight grain on pattern with selvage of fabric making sure lines are parallel. Measure the distance between selvage and pattern grain line and make sure the measurement is the same all along the grain line.

NOTCHES

Notches are used as check points when you are joining pieces together. Once you cut out your garment, clip notches at strategic points. Do this by making cuts, ¼″ long, in edge of the fabric. Strategic check points are center fronts, center backs, and any other place you feel you might need one. The cut will disappear when you make your seam. For example, if you clip a notch in the center front of the garment and the center front of the facing, you can match the notches when you put them together. Notches are noted on each pattern piece with a tiny "v."

CUTTING OUT THE GARMENT

Place all of your pattern pieces on the fabric making sure straight grain lines on the pattern are parallel to the selvage. For pieces placed on a fold, make sure fold is on the grain line.

Pin the pattern pieces in place or trace around each piece. Add seam allowances using a plastic ruler if you didn't put them on the paper pattern.

To make seam and hem allowances, lay the pattern on the fabric and draw the allowances. Allow ½″ to ¾″ for seams, and 2″ to 4″ for the hem. Make sure the allowance is the same around the entire pattern.

If you are marking directly on the fabric, make sure you are working on the wrong side of the fabric.

When two sides of a pattern are identical, only half of the pattern is given. In order to cut both sides exactly alike, fold the fabric and place the center of the pattern on the fold line of the fabric.

Straight line center fronts or backs are usually cut on the fold. If you want to make the whole pattern, simply place the center front or back of the pattern on a piece of folded paper, trace around it, and cut. Open the paper and place the whole pattern open on the open fabric. I have included a pattern layout guide with each pattern.

Cut out each piece, clipping the notches and marking any guide lines you will need for decorating.

CUTTING FACINGS

On patterns where facings are required, I have provided diagrams with a dotted line to be used as a guide. Facings and interfacings are cut exactly the same. The easiest way to cut them out is to use your cut garment as a pattern guide. Lay the cut piece on the fabric and trace around the edge. Remove cut piece and draw guide lines on the fabric for the bottom of the facing. Use a pencil or chalk, and mark the lines lightly. Wherever facings are to be joined (underarm seams, for example) the seams that will be sewn together should be the same width. Facings at seams should be approximately 1½″ to 2½″ wide. Shapes for cutting facings are suggested with the dotted lines on the illustrations.

Dotted line represents cutting line for facings

SEAMING

1. A *plain seam* is simply stitched and pressed open. The plain seam is fine for any seam that does not receive tension. For seams that break apart easily—crotch seams, for example—some type of reinforcement is needed.

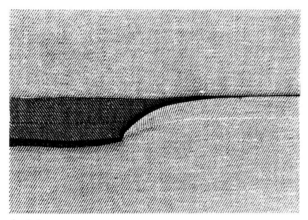

A plain seam

2. To make a *strong plain seam,* stitch two seam lines very close together. Stitch the regular seam and then stitch another parallel with it ⅛″ to ¹⁄₁₆″ away.

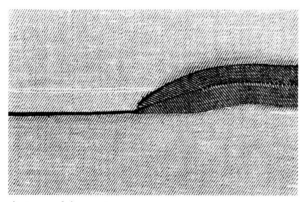

A strong plain seam

3. One of my favorite seams for strength, neatness, and appearance is a *flat feld seam.* This is the type of strong seam seen on dungarees. To make it, place the wrong sides of the fabric together and sew a plain seam. Press seam allowances to one side and trim away the under seam to ⅛″. Turn under the edge of the upper seam and pin or baste down. Stitch as close to the fold as possible.

In some cases it is difficult to make a real flat feld seam so I make a fake one. This is just as strong but isn't finished as completely on both

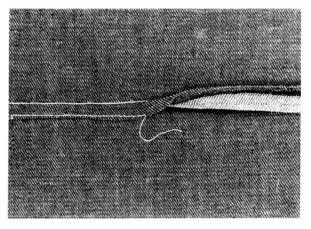

A flat feld seam

sides. To make it, sew a regular plain seam with right sides together and press seam allowances to one side. On the right side of the garment, stitch along the edge of the seam about ¹⁄₁₆″ away from the seamline. Use the width of the presser foot as your guide when sewing the second row of stitches.

4. A *french seam* is also very sturdy. It is actually two seams. Place wrong sides of the fabric together and stitch a ¼″ seam and trim as close as you can without cutting into the seam itself. Turn the fabric so the right sides are together, press along seam edge, and stitch again ¼″ from folded edge.

A French seam

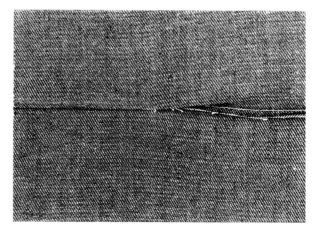

Different types of seams can be combined in the same garment. Always use a strong seam for areas that will receive stress. On a pair of overalls, for example, I combine seams by using a flat feld seam to join the center front and the center back, a fake flat feld seam for the side seams, and strong plain seams for joining the front and back inside leg.

FINISHING RAW SEAM EDGES AND HEMLINES

Seams or hemlines must often be finished to prevent fraying and unraveling. There are several ways to do this. Seams can be trimmed with pinking shears or can be finished with a straight or zig-zag stitch. The edge of a seam or hem can also be turned in ¼″ and stitched, or finished with bias tape.

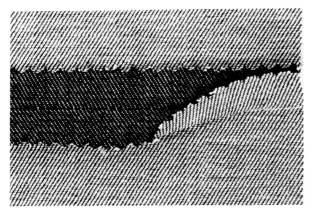

A seam trimmed with pinking shears

A stitched and pinked seam

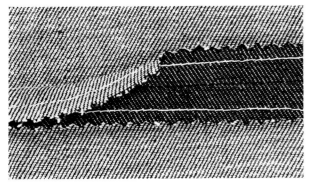

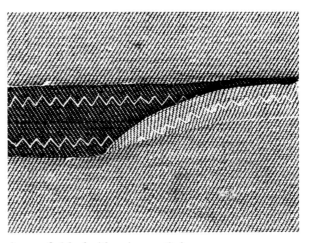

A seam finished with a zig-zag stitch

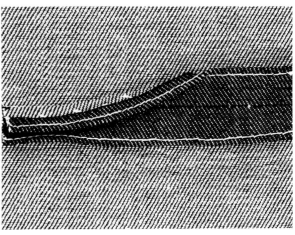

A turned and stitched seam

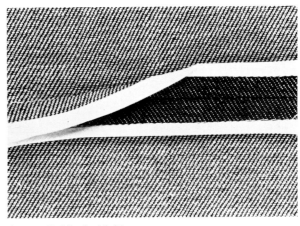

A seam finished with bias tape

The bias tape finish is especially good for hems because it is not bulky. You can cut your own bias strips or buy packages of it at any sewing supply counter or store. If you are making your own, fold your fabric on the bias and cut strips 1″ wide. If you are buying it, get the double fold ½″ wide tape.

To hem with bias tape, line up the tape with the raw edge of the hem, right sides together, and stitch.

Turn tape around the seam, press, and machine stitch the tape in place on the seamline created by the joining of the fabric and the tape.

A hem finished with bias tape

For hems, it's best to start sewing the tape on at one of the side seams. Fold the tape back ½″ at the beginning. Line up the bias tape with the raw edge of the hem, placing right sides together and using the bias fold line (¼″) as your guide line for stitching. Pull and stretch the tape around the curves of the hemline as you stitch so that some of the excess fabric will be eased in when the hem is turned back. Press tape open flat, turn it around the seam, and press. Machine stitch on the right side, on the seamline created by the joining of the fabric and the tape.

TOPSTITCHING

Topstitching, the stitching on the right side of a finished seam or edge, can be added to any garment. It gives a nice finish and keeps the pieces flat. I use topstitching on almost all garments because I love the look of it and I like the fact that it keeps everything in place through washings.

Topstitching can be done in any number of ways. Use matching or contrasting thread, or try double needle topstitching (2 rows of stitching such as that used on dungarees), or 4 or 5 rows of stitching very close together. If you have a zig-zag or fancy stitch machine the possibilities for decorative topstitching are endless. Use the zig-

Topstitching: A fake flat feld seam (left) and a real flat feld seam (right).

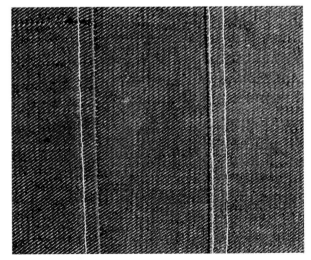

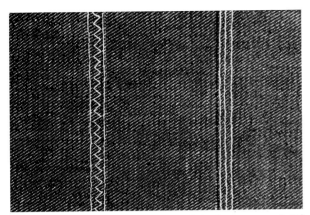

Decorative topstitching: A zig-zag stitch along a seam (left), and three rows of stitching (right).

zag stitch along a seam in contrasting thread or experiment with any of the other stitches. The best thing about topstitching is that it is both utilitarian as well as decorative.

SEWING TIPS

Certain things can be done to make your sewing easier. The following are a few tips I have learned along the way and want to pass on to you. As you go along, you, too, will find shortcuts and ways to do things that make your work faster and easier.

Good sharp scissors are essential. There is nothing more frustrating than working with dull scissors that chew fabric and break your arm and spirit. Keep one pair for sewing and allow them to be used *only* for cutting fabric or thread. Don't allow them to be used for paper; this dulls them very quickly. Small sharp scissors are good to keep by the machine so that you can trim threads off the seams as you are sewing.

A large flat work table will make pattern and fabric cutting easier. If you have the room, an unfinished door is a cheap and ideal surface for laying out fabric and cutting patterns. You can place the door on a small table to hold it, or buy legs and attach them. If you're not lucky enough to have room for this, lay fabric and pattern out on the floor making sure the floor is clean. Always try to lay fabric or paper flat.

When you have your sewing machine set up, have your iron and ironing board ready also. One is as important as the other. Pressing as you go

along will save time and make your work neater and easier. Seams should always be pressed open or closed; pockets and facings should be pressed before they are applied. In many cases, ironing can take the place of pinning or basting by keeping things flat and in place. A good general rule is to always press as you go.

If you are a beginner, you may feel you have to baste. I suggest you pin or press instead. If pins are put perpendicular to the line or seam to be stitched, they will hold securely and you can, with most machines, stitch right over them. You can also stitch along and pull each pin out as you reach it. Keep a pincushion handy so that you can replace pins in it as you go and they won't end up all over your machine or floor. Some will inevitably fall, so keep a small magnet handy to gather them up easily.

It's a good idea to trim seams fairly close as you go along so the garment isn't bulky with excess seam allowance. Clipping corners off and making small clips in the seams along curves will make seams neater and make turning facings easier. Trim a seam that will not show to ¼″ or less, though be sure to leave enough fabric so that the seam won't pull out.

Get all of your materials together before you sit down to sew. I like to finish a garment in one sitting and there is nothing more frustrating than not having all the supplies I need to complete it. Make sure you have thread, zippers, buttons, or whatever notions you might need before you start sewing.

GLOSSARY OF TERMS

BIAS OF A FABRIC. This is the direction that is at a 45° angle to the straight and cross grain of the fabric. The bias line always has stretch.

BIAS TAPE. This can be cut from the fabric itself in bias strips or can be purchased at any sewing supply or dime store. Buy ½″ single folded bias tape or bias binding for all projects. It is used for clean finishing edges.

FACING. A facing is a lining cut in a shape corresponding to the edges of a garment. It is applied so that edges such as necklines or armholes will be finished clean.

GRAIN LINES. Grain lines are the directions the threads run in a woven fabric. STRAIGHT GRAIN is the direction of threads in the fabric running parallel with the selvage or length of the fabric. CROSS GRAIN is the direction of threads in the fabric running at right angles to the straight grain.

INTERFACING. An interfacing is a lightweight fabric sewn between two layers of fabric to stiffen or strengthen an area. It is often cut in the same shape as the facing.

NAP. The nap of the fabric is composed of the short fibers on the surface of the fabric that give it a one-way direction. For example, velvet and corduroy have a one-way nap. All pieces of a garment should be cut so that any nap goes in the same direction.

NOTCHES. A notch is a ¼″ cut in the seam allowance and is used as a guide line when joining pieces of the garment.

SELVAGE. The selvages are the finished edges running along the length of a woven fabric.

SIDES. The *right side* is the front or face of the fabric that is to be the outside of the finished garment. The *wrong side* is the back or reverse side of the fabric that is to be on the inside of the finished garment.

STAY STITCH. Stay stitching is a straight row of machine stitches made slightly in from the edge of a garment piece. It is used on raw necklines and armholes so that they don't stretch out of shape while the garment is being worked.

TACKING. Tacking is several stitches made in the same place to reinforce a point of stress. On the machine it can be done by going back and forth for a few stitches.

The
Patterns

FABRIC REQUIREMENTS

Fabric requirements are given for each basic pattern with seam allowances, facings, and 3″ hems. If you want extra-long lengths, allow for more fabric when you buy it. Pockets will generally fit in between the spaces of the pattern pieces, but if you want extra-large pockets, also add more yardage to the given measurement. If you decide to cut large pockets after you've already purchased the fabric, cut the facings in contrasting fabric and use the fabric allotted for the facings of the pockets instead.

Most fabrics suitable for children's clothes come in 44–45″ widths, but you can also buy fabric in widths of 35–36″ and 59–60″. Estimated yardage is given for 35–36″ fabrics and for 44–45″. For 59–60″ fabric, use the 44–45″ yardage requirement. A good general rule when buying fabric is to buy ⅛ to ¼ yard more than the total length of the garment. (Measure from the shoulder to the hemline on the child.)

PATTERN LAYOUT ON FABRIC

The suggested pattern layouts on fabric are given for 44–45″ widths because this is the most common width. Use these as a guide for all widths, but lay all the pattern pieces on fabric before you start cutting so you are sure to have enough. The layouts I have suggested allow room for pockets and give you a little extra fabric to play with.

You can make your own layout or rearrange the pattern pieces in order to save fabric. Just remember to cut the required number of pieces specified on each pattern piece. In some cases such as waistbands, suspenders, or pockets, you can change grain lines. Also you can cut facings in another fabric.

Button Shoulder Dress and Jumpsuit

These classic button shoulder garments, made either as a dress or a jumpsuit, look adorable on any child, and because of their simplicity are easy and fun to decorate. These garments can be worn as cool summer clothes when made in lightweight fabrics, or as winter clothes, with a turtleneck sweater or shirt. Either style can be cut long or short, and the button shoulder pants look just as cute on little girls as they do on boys. These styles make ideal brother and sister outfits. (See the Sunbonnet Sue and Calico Bill appliqué patterns.) A pattern for a pair of bloomers is included to go under the dress.

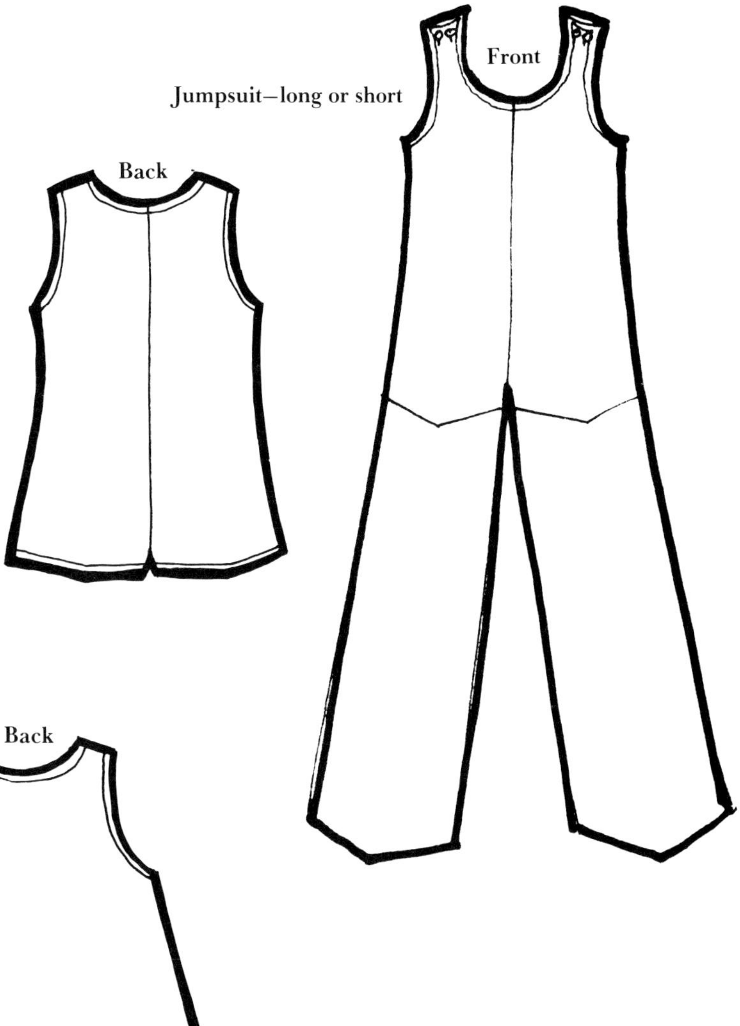

Jumpsuit—long or short

Back

Front

Front

Dress & bloomers

Back

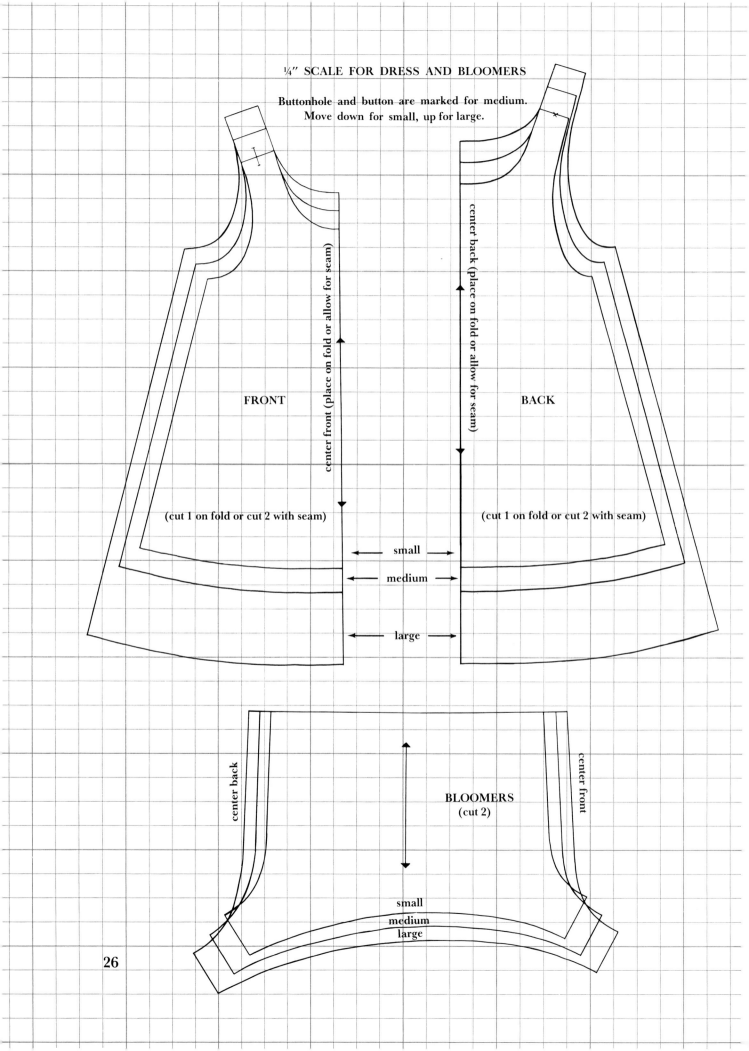

¼″ SCALE FOR DRESS AND BLOOMERS

Buttonhole and button are marked for medium.
Move down for small, up for large.

FRONT

center front (place on fold or allow for seam)

(cut 1 on fold or cut 2 with seam)

BACK

center back (place on fold or allow for seam)

(cut 1 on fold or cut 2 with seam)

small

medium

large

center back

BLOOMERS
(cut 2)

center front

small
medium
large

26

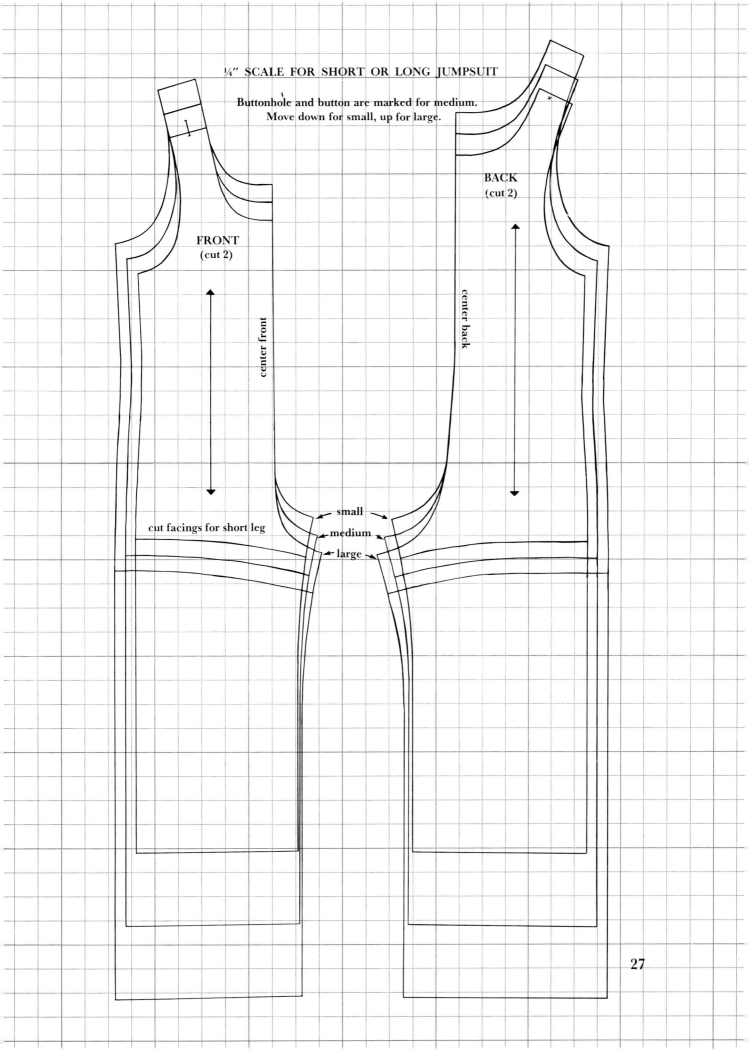

¼″ SCALE FOR SHORT OR LONG JUMPSUIT

Buttonhole and button are marked for medium.
Move down for small, up for large.

FRONT
(cut 2)

center front

BACK
(cut 2)

center back

cut facings for short leg

small

medium

large

27

Center front zipper

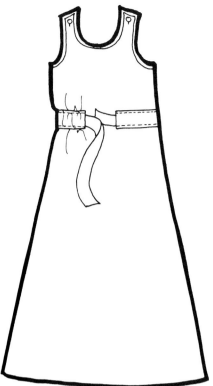

Cut long with waistline casing and tie

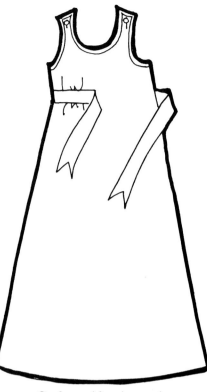

Cut long with a tie at waist

Center back opening with ties

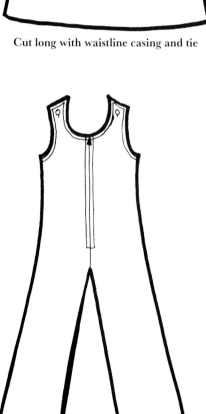

Cut long with zipper in front

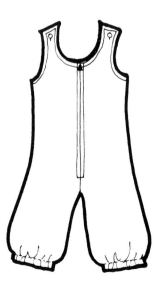

Cut for knickers with elastic
through turnback at knee

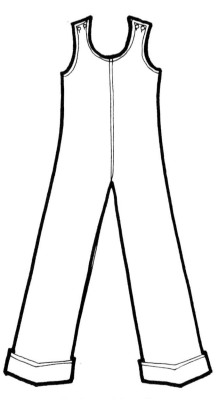

Cut long with cuffs

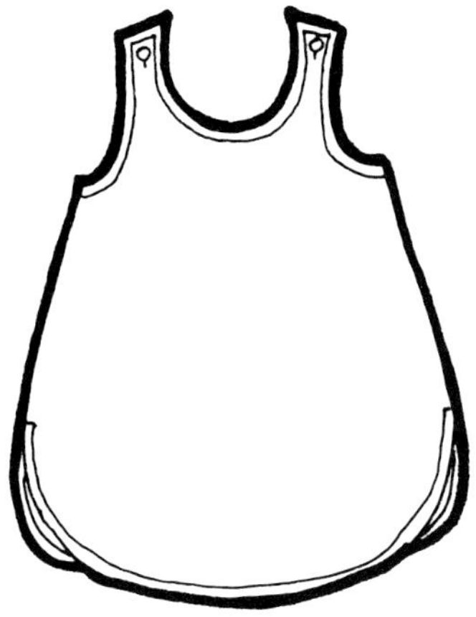

Reshaped hemline with curve at sides

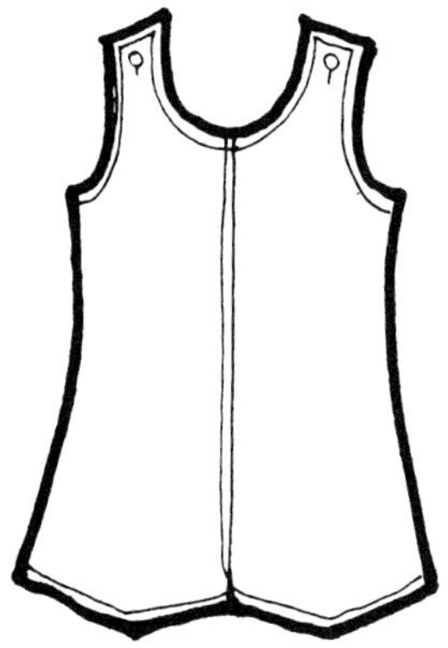

Cut short

FABRIC REQUIREMENTS AND LAYOUTS

		SMALL	MED-LARGE
Dress	35–36″	1¼ yd.	1⅝ yd.
	44–45″	¾ yd.	1 yd.
Bloomers	35–36″		
	44–45″	⅜ yd. all widths & sizes	
Jumpsuit (long)	35–36″	2¼ yd.	2½ yd.
	44–45″	1¼ yd.	1½ yd.
Jumpsuit (short)	35–36″	1¼ yd.	1⅜ yd.
	44–45″	¾ yd.	1 yd.

PATTERN LAYOUTS ON 44-45″ FABRIC

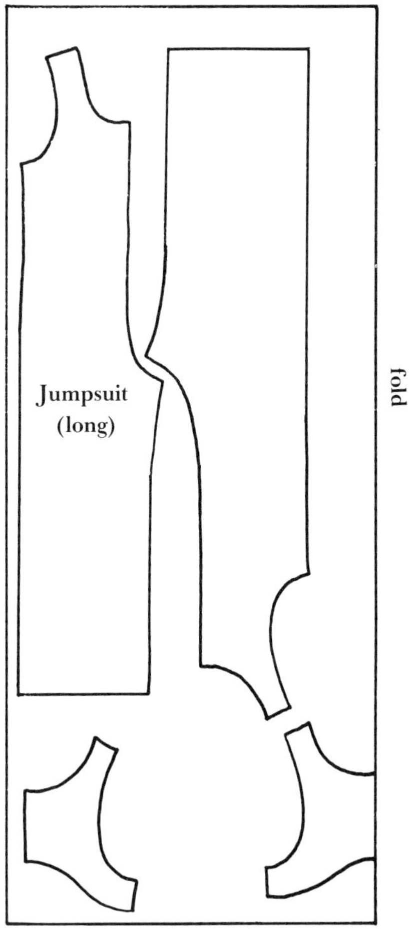

SEWING SUPPLIES

1. *Fabric*
2. *Thread:* Contrasting or matching color
3. *Interfacing:* ¼ yard lightweight
4. *Single fold bias tape:* 1 package, ½″ wide
5. *Buttons:* 2 buttons ⅝″, or 4 buttons ¼″
6. *Zipper:* If you want garment to zip open down the front,
   10″ zipper—small
   12″ zipper—medium
   14″ zipper—large
7. *Elastic* for bloomers: ¼″ wide (1½ yds.)

Dress

fold

fold

Bloomers

fold

selvages

Jumpsuit (short)

selvages

fold

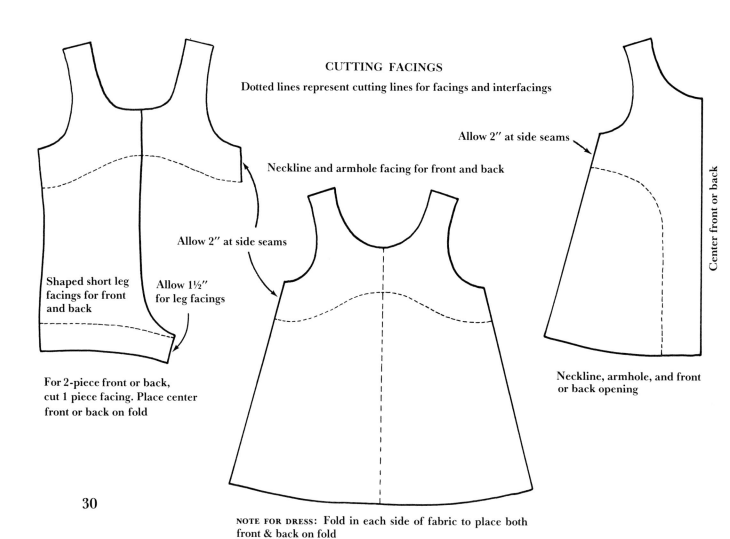

CUTTING FACINGS

Dotted lines represent cutting lines for facings and interfacings

Allow 2″ at side seams

Neckline and armhole facing for front and back

Allow 2″ at side seams

Allow 1½″ for leg facings

Shaped short leg facings for front and back

For 2-piece front or back, cut 1 piece facing. Place center front or back on fold

Center front or back

Neckline, armhole, and front or back opening

NOTE FOR DRESS: Fold in each side of fabric to place both front & back on fold

30

ASSEMBLING THE DRESS AND JUMPSUIT

1. Scale the pattern up to size, add seam and hem allowances, and cut out the garment in fabric. Cut out facings and/or pockets if you wish. Mark the center front of the dress with a basting line of thread. Join the center front seam of the pants before applying any decoration. The basting line or seam line is a guide line for decoration. Stay stitch armholes and neckline ½″ away from the edge if you feel you might stretch them while you're decorating. If you are not going to decorate the garment, simply proceed with the instructions for sewing together. Otherwise, decorate the piece or pieces and then sew the garment together.

2. *Optional zip front opening.* Place the right sides of the front together and join starting ½″ below the bottom of the zipper (10½, 12½, 14½″). Clip seam at curve and press entire front seam open. Starting about 1″ down from the neckline, line up the center of the zipper with the center opening and baste or pin the zipper in place. If you want the teeth of the zipper exposed, press back more seam allowance (about ⅛″ more on each side). For a covered zipper, stitch ⅜″ away from the center line all around. For an exposed zipper, stitch close to the edge.

For zip front opening on pants, place right sides together and starting ½″ below the bottom of the zipper, stitch seam together at the crotch. Clip seam.

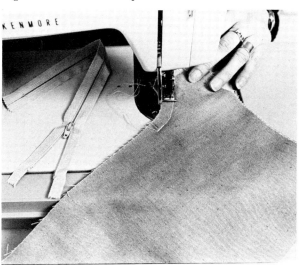

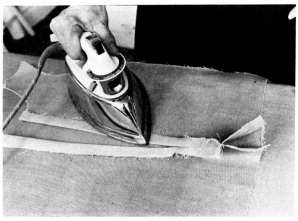

Press entire front seam open.

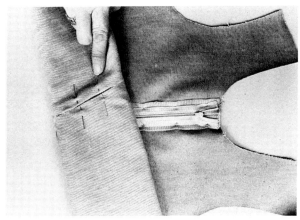

Line the center of the zipper with the opening and baste or pin the zipper in place.

For a covered zipper, stitch ⅜″ away from the center line.

31

For an exposed zipper, stitch very close to the center line.

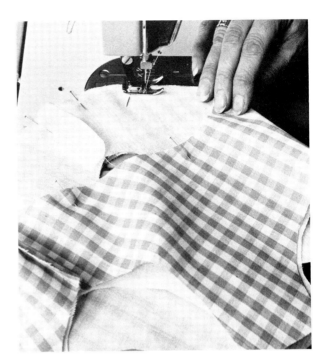

To join the facing to the interfacing, place right sides together and stitch around the bottom edge.

3. Join the center back seam of the pants body. For both garments, join the side seams of garment itself, the facings, and the interfacings. Trim, press seams open.

For the neckline facings, join the side seams of the facings and the interfacings.

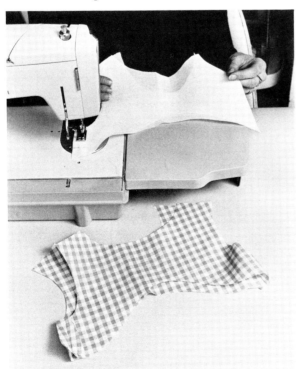

4. Join neckline facing and interfacing together by placing right sides together and stitching seam around the bottom edge. As you sew, match up notches and side seams. Trim seam close, turn, and press. For short pant leg facings, join side seams and inside leg seams of facings and of interfacings. With right sides together, join facings to interfacings around the top. Turn and press.

Turn facing right side out and press.

These button-shoulder styles are made in seersucker and
appliquéd with the "Sunbonnet Sue" and "Calico Bill" designs.

*The button-shoulder dress is made in gray flannel and appliquéd
with the "Patchwork House" design. The boy's tartan wool pants
are made from the overalls pattern and his gray flannel jacket
is lined with the same wool tartan material. His sweater is made
from the fisherman's knit pattern.*

5. For pants body, join front and back inside leg seam together, matching center front and back seams. Sew on pant leg facings/interfacings by placing right sides together and stitching around leg openings. Turn and press.

After joining leg facing to leg interfacing, attach facing to leg opening, right sides together.

6. To join facing/interfacing to neckline, pin right sides together matching notches and side seams. Starting at one of the side seams (or at the center front for zipper style), stitch around entire neckline and armhole openings. Trim seam allowance to ¼″, clip the curves, turn, and press. For zipper style, turn in facings edges around zipper and catch by hand. Add topstitching if you wish. Facings can be tacked down by hand on the inside at the seams so they will stay down. NOTE: When turning pieces with corners or points, use a pin to pull them out on the right side.

To attach neckline facing to garment, place right sides together matching side seams and notches. Stitch around entire neckline, trim, turn, and press.

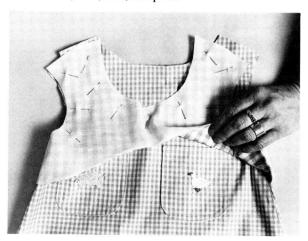

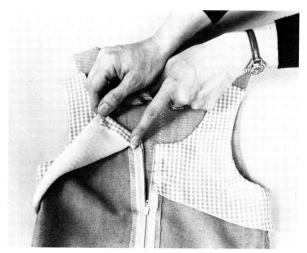

For zipper style, turn in facing edges around the zipper and catch by hand.

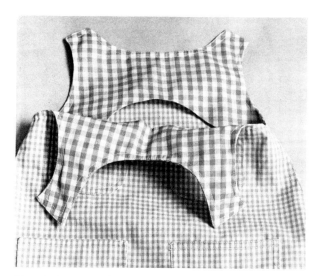

Topstitch the neckline facing, if you wish.

When turning pieces with corners or points, use a pin to pull excess fabric out on the right side.

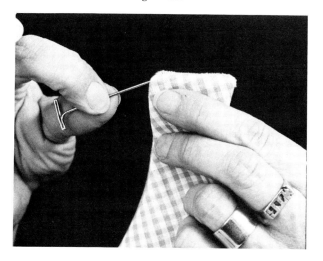

7. Finish clean the raw hem of the dress by either turning under ¼″ and stitching or using bias tape. (See seams section.) Turn up hem and pin all around evenly. Ease in any fullness. Stitch by hand or machine.

8. Make one or two buttonholes on the front of each shoulder and sew the buttons on the back shoulders.

ASSEMBLING THE BLOOMERS

1. Scale pattern up to size, add ¾″ seam allowances at waistline and leg bottoms and ½″ seam for center front and back seams. Cut out in fabric.

2. Place right sides together and join front and back center seams.

3. Join front to back at crotch matching center front and back seams.

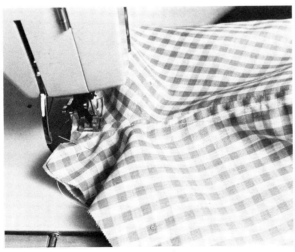

On bloomers, join the front to the back at the crotch, matching center front and back seams.

4. Turn under ¼″ at waist and leg openings and press. To make casings, turn back ½″, press, and stitch the edge by machine, leaving an opening at side seam so the elastic can be pulled through.

5. Insert elastic in waist and leg casings. This can be done by putting a small safety pin on one end of the elastic and running it through. Adjust elastic to fit, lap ends over, and stitch. Stitch openings closed.

To insert elastic into casing, put a small safety pin on one end of the elastic and run it through the casing.

ELASTIC CHART

	SMALL	MEDIUM	LARGE
Waist (cut 1)	17½″	19″	21″
Legs (cut 2)	9½″	11″	13″

Bibbed Overalls (Sunsuit, Jumper, Pants, Shorts, Skirt)

This pattern, with minor adjustments, can serve many different purposes. The basic overalls look terrific on both boys and girls. Cut with shorts, it's a great sunsuit; cut with a skirt, it's a sundress or overall jumper. The bib is the perfect spot for embroidered or appliquéd decoration. For real tailoring, lots of pockets and topstitching can be applied. You can also eliminate the bib and make pull-on pants, shorts, or a simple skirt.

Shorts (back)

Cut with skirt for jumper

Long pant with cuff

Short sunsuit

Short skirt

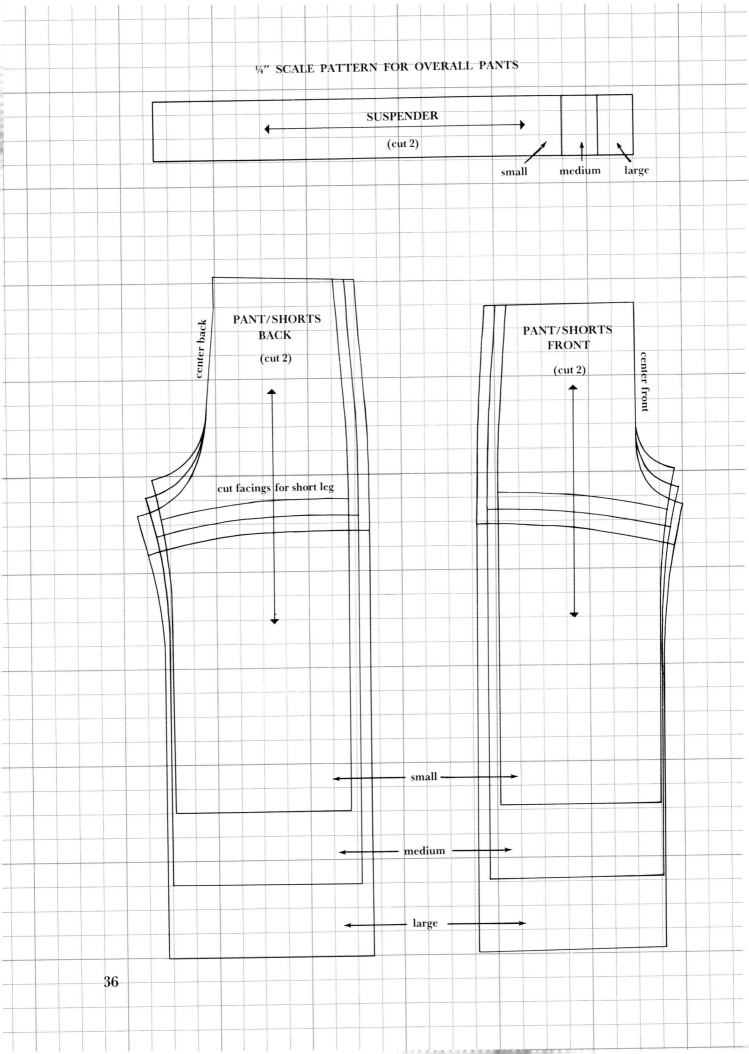

¼″ SCALE PATTERN FOR OVERALL PANTS

SUSPENDER

(cut 2)

small   medium   large

PANT/SHORTS
BACK

(cut 2)

center back

cut facings for short leg

PANT/SHORTS
FRONT

(cut 2)

center front

small

medium

large

36

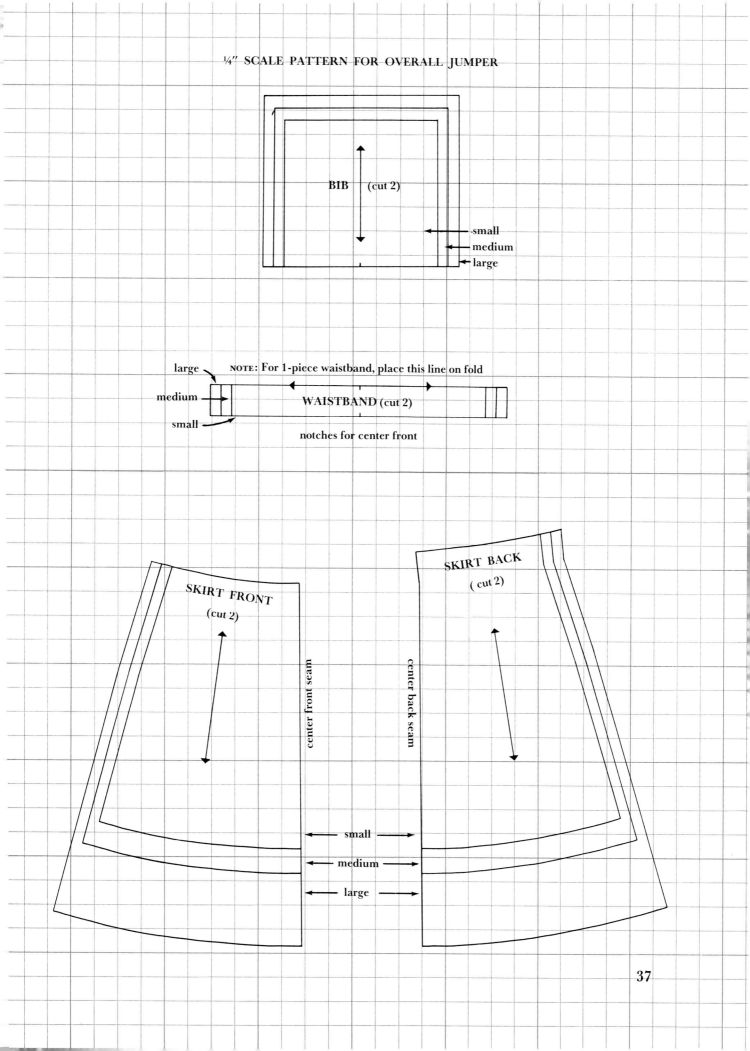

SEWING SUPPLIES

1. *Fabric*
2. *Thread:* contrasting or matching
3. *Elastic:* ⅝″–¾″ wide (½ yard)
4. *Buttons for straps:* 2 buttons ⅝″ wide
5. *Bias tape:* ½″ wide single fold for finishing seams or back of waistline of pants. (Optional)

FABRIC REQUIREMENTS AND LAYOUTS

SIZES

	FABRIC WIDTH	SMALL	MED-LARGE
Overalls (long)	35–36″	1½ yd.	1¾ yd.
	44–45″	1 yd.	1¼ yd.
Overalls (short)	35–36″	¾ yd.	1 yd.
(sunsuit)	44–45″	⅝ yd.	¾ yd.
Overall jumper	35–36″	1 yd.	1¼ yd.
(with skirt)	44–45″	¾ yd.	1 yd.
Pants	35–36″	1½ yd.	1¾ yd.
	44–45″	¾ yd.	1 yd.
Shorts	35–36″	½ yd.	¾ yd.
	44–45″	⅜ yd.	½ yd.
Skirt	35–36″	1 yd.	1⅛ yd.
	44–45″	⅜ yd.	⅝ yd.

PATTERN LAYOUTS ON 44–45″ FABRIC

Skirt

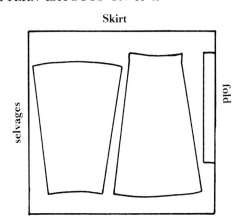

Overall jumper

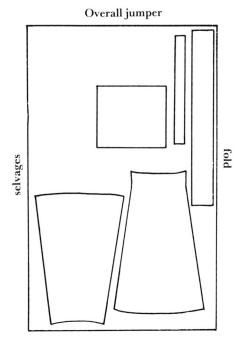

Shorts

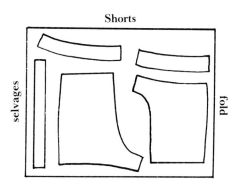

Overalls (long)

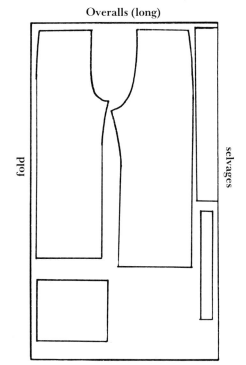

Pants

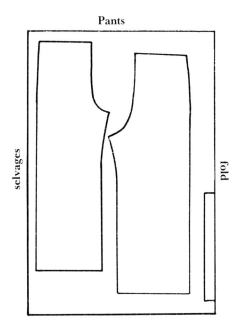

Overalls (short sunsuit)

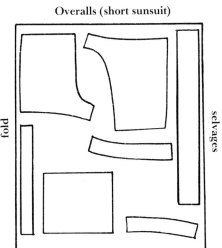

ASSEMBLING THE OVERALLS

1. Scale the pattern up to size and add seam and hem or cuff allowances. Add 1½″ at the top of the back waistline for casing for elastic. If you intend to make just pants, shorts, or a skirt without the bib, cut the waistband with the top along a fold and add seam allowances on the three other sides. Cut facings and interfacings for short pants and pockets if you wish. Mark center front of the bib as a guideline for any decoration. (If you intend to do embroidery using a hoop, cut the bib about

3″ larger on each side. This allows you to have enough excess fabric to fit around the hoop. Once the decoration has been completed, cut the bib down to size.)

Once you have decorated the piece or pieces, join the garment together.

2. Join center front and back seams of pants or skirt.

3. Join bib to bib facing by placing right sides together and stitching around the top and two sides. Leave the bottom open so it can be turned. Trim seams, clip off corners, turn, and press. Topstitch around three sides if desired.

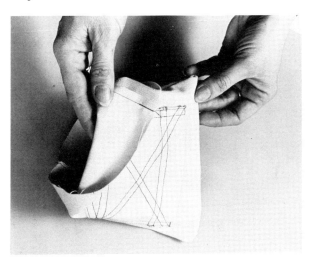

Join bib to bib facing by placing right sides together and stitching around three sides, leaving the bottom open.

4. Join bib to waistband by placing bib in the center front, between the front and back of waistband. (Right sides of the waistbands should

Join bib to waistband by placing bib between the front and the back of the waistband pieces.

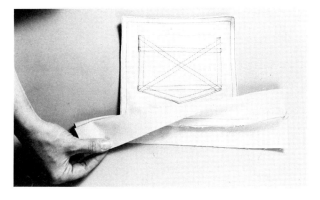

be facing each other.) Line up the edge of bib with the edges of the waistbands and stitch across. Trim seams and press waistbands down.

5. To join bib and waistband to pant front, place the *right* side of the back waistband to the *wrong* side of the pants front. Stitch, trim seam, and press. Press back the seam allowance of the front waistband so it is even and flat with the back waistband. Pin or baste, and topstitch along the edge of the pressed back seam. The front of the garment is now finished.

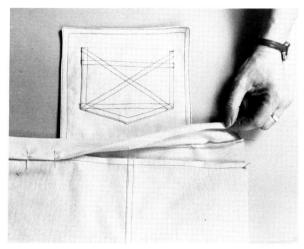

To join bib and waistband to pant front, place the right side of the back waistband to the wrong side of the pants front.

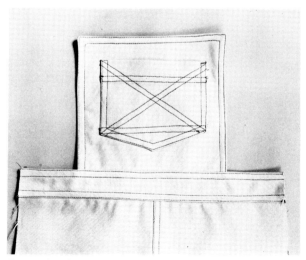

A completed overall front with topstitching

If you are not making a bib, place the right side of the back of the *one-piece* waistband to wrong side of pants or skirt front. Stitch, trim,

press up seam allowances, and press waistband along fold line. Turn back seam allowance, press, and stitch on the right side.

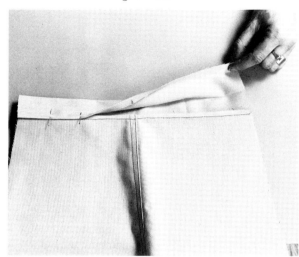

If making a skirt or pants without a bib, be sure to cut a one-piece waistband.

6. Clean finish upper edge of back pants or skirt by pressing back ¼″ seam and stitching or by using bias tape. (See "Finishing Raw Edges and Hemlines," page 21.) Fold edge back 1″ (1½″ if you use bias tape finish) and press. This will be the casing for the elastic. Pin elastic to the back at each end of casing, placing it 1″ in from each side seam and lining it up with the fold line. Stitch each end by machine securely.

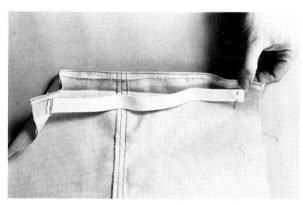

For back of overalls, pin elastic to the back at each end of the casing. Stitch each end securely.

Guide for Elastic (⅝″–¾″ wide)
    small—8″
    medium—9″
    large—10½″

7. To join side seams, place right side of front and back together lining up the top of front waistband with the fold line on back. Starting at the top, stitch the side seam closed. Turn back casing over front, pin in place, and stitch down. Turn casing toward back and press the entire seam to back. Trim seams if they are too bulky.

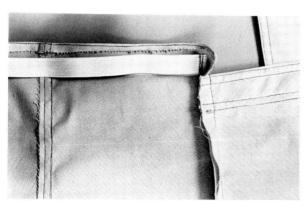

To join side seams, place right side of front and back together, lining up the top of front waistband with the fold line on the back.

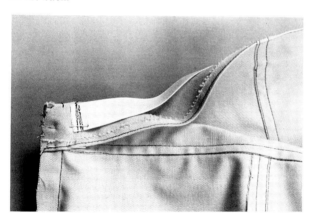

Turn back casing over front, pin, and stitch down.

Turn casing toward back and press the entire seam.

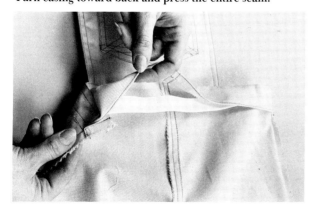

8. Stretch and pin the elastic in place at about 3 points across the back to hold it while stitching. Stitch the casing closed by stretching out the elastic and stitching along the edge of the casing. Be careful not to catch the elastic in the stitching. Join the inside leg seams together, if you are making pants.

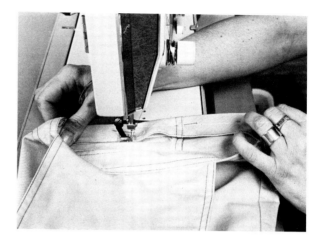

Stitch along the edge of the casing, being careful not to catch the elastic in the stitching.

9. *Suspenders.* Right sides together, fold suspender in half lengthwise and stitch seam. Trim and press seam open keeping seam in center as you press. This step makes the turning easier. Using a pencil or stick, turn the suspender by pushing it through itself. Press again, keeping seam in center. Turn in raw edges at each end and press. Slip stitch ends closed and topstitch, if you wish.

When pressing suspender seams, be sure to keep seam in the center as you press.

Using a pencil or stick, turn the suspender inside out by pushing it through itself.

Attach the suspenders to the pants back by either stitching them in place or securing them with a button and buttonhole.

10. Make one buttonhole on one end of each strap and one on each side of the bib. Sew button to inside of back, placing each button in the middle of each side of the back. Button strap to back and bring to front. Adjust and mark for button on strap front. (If you wish, simply stitch the suspenders to the inside back along the stitching line at the edge of the casing.)

11. Clean finish raw hem of pants, turn up evenly, and hem by hand or machine.

12. For short pants, join side seams of both the facings and the interfacings. Stitch facing to interfacing, placing right sides together and stitching around the top. Turn and press. Join facings to leg edge, turn, and press. Secure facing in place by hand or machine.

Jacket (Tunic, Coat, Smock, Bathrobe)

This pattern can be used for virtually any kind of a coverup you would like. It can be a jacket or coat with a zip front, a smock that ties front or back for painting or just keeping your child clean, a big roomy play shirt, or a bathrobe, made simply by extending the pattern to the floor. It's cut full so that it will fit easily over other clothes and be comfortable. This basic pattern can become the special accessory piece you will want to make just for fun.

Fabric is especially important for this garment. It can be completely lined, and can even be reversible, if you use a reversible zipper. Try cutting the outside of a jacket or coat in wool and using a furry pile fabric for lining. Or use cotton with a terry cloth lining for a bath or beach robe and cut it long or short. Try tough denim for a smock, or cut the smock longer for a little girl to wear with a turtleneck and tights as a smock dress.

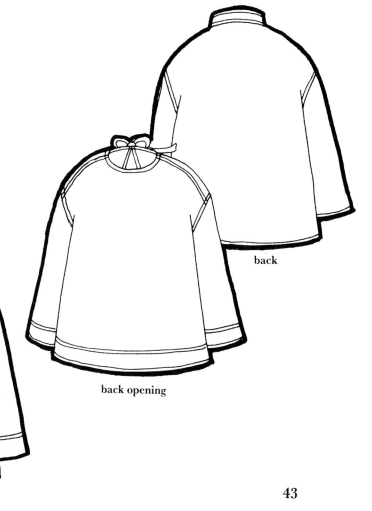

back

back opening

front opening

VARIATIONS ON JACKET PATTERN

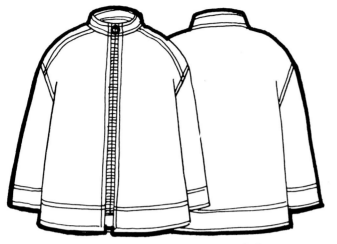

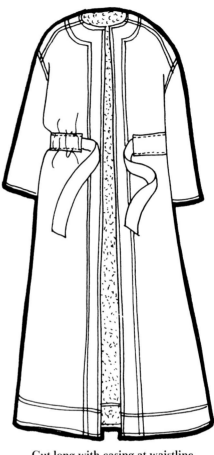

Center front seam with zipper for jacket

Smock with center back opening and ties

Cut long with casing at waistline
for tie-robe or beachcoat

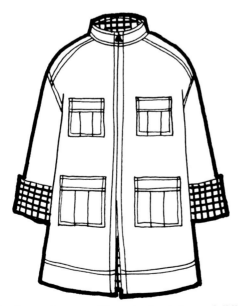

Cut longer for coat with center front zipper, full lining,
and turnback cuff

Cut dress length with tie back and
elastic at bottom of sleeve

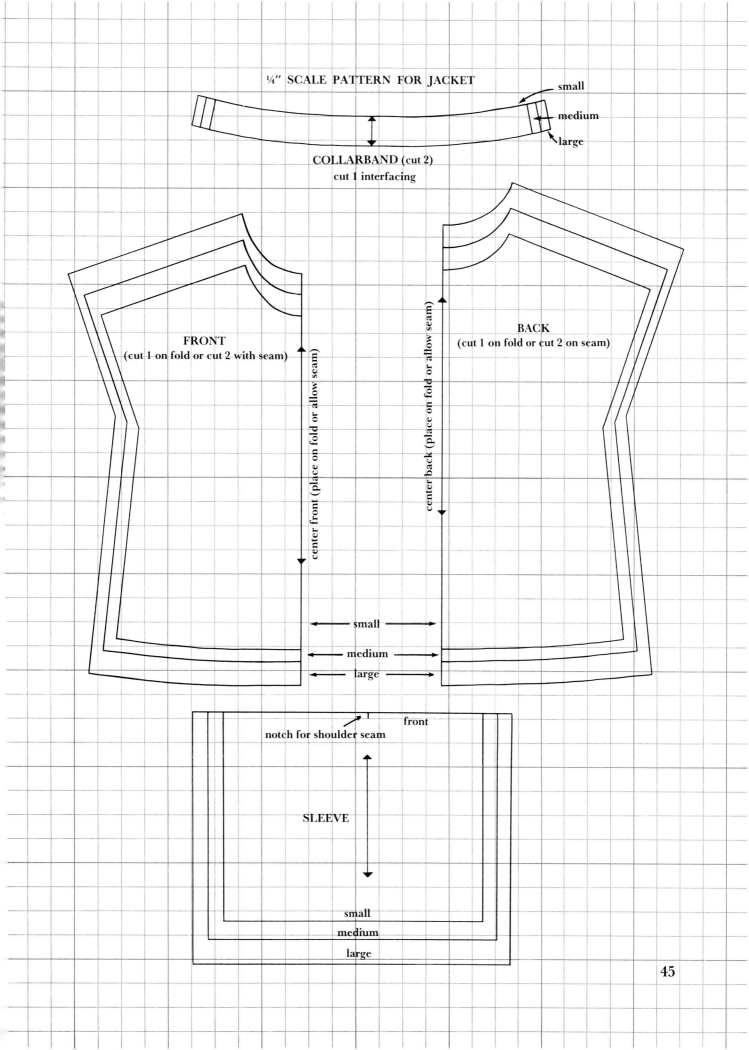

¼″ SCALE PATTERN FOR JACKET

small

medium

large

COLLARBAND (cut 2)
cut 1 interfacing

FRONT
(cut 1 on fold or cut 2 with seam)

center front (place on fold or allow seam)

BACK
(cut 1 on fold or cut 2 on seam)

center back (place on fold or allow seam)

small

medium

large

notch for shoulder seam

front

SLEEVE

small

medium

large

45

SEWING SUPPLIES

1. *Fabric* and *interfacing*
2. *Thread:* contrasting or matching
3. *Self or ribbon ties:* Each about 14″ long or 3 yards per garment (Optional)
4. Separating *zipper* for jacket:
   12″—small
   14″—medium
   16″—large
   (longer for coat)

FABRIC REQUIREMENTS AND LAYOUT

	FABRIC WIDTH	SMALL	MED-LARGE
Jacket	35–36″	1½ yd.	1¾ yd.
	44–45″	1¼ yd.	1½ yd.

NOTE: Hold paper pattern up to child and see if you want to cut it longer. If you do, add the length to the fabric requirement. Also add fabric if you want big pockets.

JACKET LAYOUT ON 44-45″ FABRIC

selvages

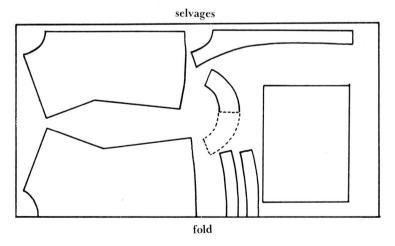

fold

NOTE: Place either center front or center back on fold.

CUTTING FACINGS FOR JACKET

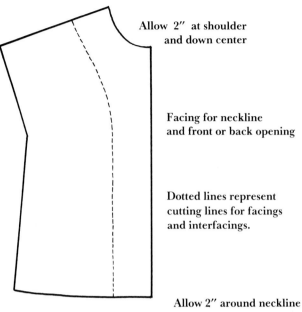

Allow 2″ at shoulder and down center

Facing for neckline and front or back opening

Dotted lines represent cutting lines for facings and interfacings.

Allow 2″ around neckline

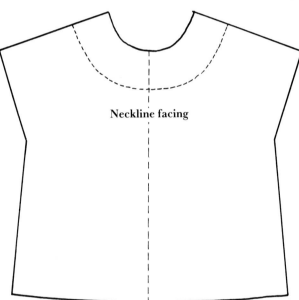

Neckline facing

ASSEMBLING THE JACKET

1. Scale the pattern up to size, adding the seam and hem allowances. Add to the sleeve length if you want cuffs and to the front or back if you want overlapping. Cut facings, pockets, tie belts, ties, or anything else you might want. Add ½″

seam allowance on each side of the center front (more for an overlap) and place the center back on the fold of the pattern. Do the opposite for back opening. You can also make it a pullover garment by placing both front and back on folds and then cutting the center front or back as far down as you want and facing it. Cut a collarband, if you wish, placing band on center front or back fold to match garment. Decorate the pieces if you wish and then join the garment together.

NOTE: If you want to make narrow self ties for closing, cut strips of fabric along straight grain 1″ wide. Press in each edge about ¼″ with iron. Fold strip in half and press again. Stitch along edge by machine. Cut individual ties from one long strip and finish edges by stitching back and forth so the tie ends won't unravel.

To make narrow self-ties, cut strips of fabric, press in each edge with an iron, fold strip in half, and stitch.

2. Placing right sides together, join shoulder seams. Press seam allowance toward back and topstitch. (This is a good place for a⋅ flat fed seam.)

Joining shoulder seams

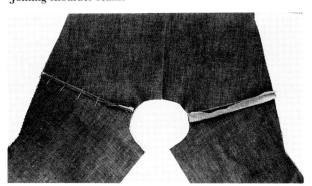

3. *Collarband style* (with or without zipper). Placing right sides together, join collarbands and interfacing, keeping interfacing on top of one side. If there is a zipper, seam across top of collarband only. If not, stitch seams of collarband center fronts (or backs) along with the top. Trim seams, turn, and press. Stitch *top* (or outside) collarband to neck edge, placing right sides together and matching notches. Trim seams, press seam allowances toward top of collarband. Turn back edges of *under* collarband so it's even with stitched line and sew by hand or machine.

Joining collarbands, keeping interfacing on the top of one side.

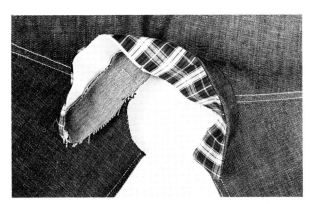

To join collarband to neck edge, first stitch right side of band to right side of neck edge.

Turn inside of collarband so that it is even with the stitched line and stitch by hand or machine.

3a. *Zipper.* Put in a zipper before the collarband is finished. Pin or baste the closed zipper in place starting at the top of each side. Stitch by machine. Once zipper is stitched in, turn collarband down folding back all the rough edges and pinning so that the band stays flat. Stitch by hand or machine. Topstitch the band if you wish.

To insert zipper, pin or baste the closed zipper to the edge of the opening. Machine stitch into place.

4. *Tie or Wrap style.* Join facings and interfacings together. (See page 34.) To join facings to garment, place right sides together and match shoulder seams. Stitch, trim seams, turn, and press. NOTE: If you want ties for closing, insert them between the garment and the facing, or put them on after the garment is finished. Use as many as you wish, making sure to place them evenly on each side.

A tie inserted between the garment and the facing.

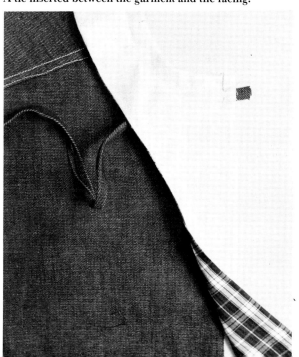

5. Placing right sides together, join sleeve to body, matching shoulder seam and notch. Press seam allowances toward bottom of sleeve and topstitch armhole seam.

Join sleeve to body, matching shoulder seam and notch.

Topstitch armhole seam.

6. Close side seam placing right sides together and stitching a curved line at the underarm point. Clip the seam at the curve and press open.

Stitch a curved line at the underarm and clip.

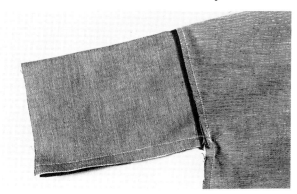

7. Hem the sleeve and the bottom of garment all around evenly; stitch by hand or machine. Add topstitching if you wish.

Lining the Jacket

1. To line a coat or jacket, cut out and assemble 2 complete garments, joining shoulder seams, sleeves, and side seams. (No facings are needed because the garments will be joined at the edges.)

A lined jacket. Note that no facings are needed.

2. If it has a collarband, join band at neck edge of each garment. Place right sides together and stitch across top of the collarband. Turn and press. Proceed with the zipper (See page 48), keeping the lining loose. Stitch zipper to the outer garment and then turn back lining on inside so that it is not in the way of the zipper and stitch by hand or machine.

3. If there is no collarband or zipper, simply place right sides together, and stitch around front or back opening and neckline. Turn and press. Insert ties in the seam or sew them on after.

4. Turn in sleeve and bottom openings evenly on both the outside and the lining. Stitch together by hand or machine.

Casing for a Tie

If you want to make a casing for a tie-front garment, after side seams have been joined, try the garment on and tie a string where you want the casing to go. Mark tie line with chalk or pins. Measure the length of the line you've marked and cut a 2″-wide strip of fabric, on the bias, 3″ less than the measurement. (You can cut the strip on the straight, but it will not lie as flat.) Press in ¼″ on each side of strip, and ½″ on each end. Stitch ends closed. Starting 2″ away from the center front, lay the strip on garment and pin down in center all around. Stitch close to edge on each side of strip to secure it to the garment. Pull self-tie or ribbon through casing with a safety pin.

A casing for a tie-front garment.

Sweaters

There is something very special about a hand-knitted sweater. A style that works well with all the basic patterns in this book is a long-sleeved turtleneck (or crew neck) sweater. You can make this sweater solid or striped, in a plain Stockinette stitch using a sport-weight yarn. This sweater looks great under the button shoulder garments and is perfect with the overalls and jumper.

Try making the sweater so that it will go with several different pants or skirts. A striped sweater is ideal for this purpose. For example, a red and navy striped sweater can be worn with either red, navy, or white pants or skirts. Combine four or more colors in stripes and make it even more flexible. If you really love color you might want to

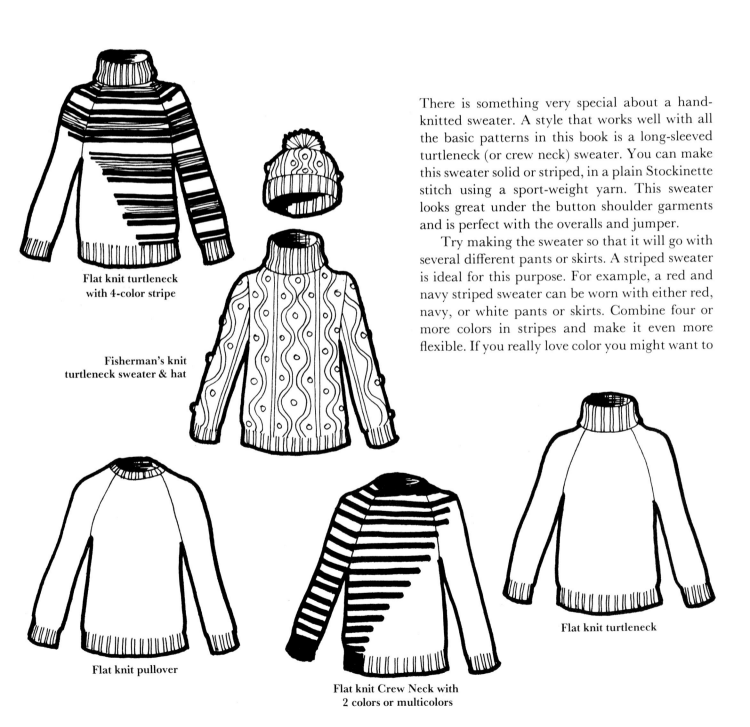

Flat knit turtleneck
with 4-color stripe

Fisherman's knit
turtleneck sweater & hat

Flat knit pullover

Flat knit Crew Neck with
2 colors or multicolors

Flat knit turtleneck

try making each stripe a different color. Just make sure that sleeves and side seams match up where they meet at the armhole. There are three stripe patterns suggested, so experiment with different color combinations. Make up your own stripe patterns if you like.

I have also included a pattern for a fisherman's knit sweater. This pattern is more complicated, but the results are well worth the effort. It can be made with regular knitting worsted, and is perfect to use in place of a jacket. A hat pattern is included to go along with it.

Natural wool is classic for the fisherman's sweater, but try it in a cherry red, a yellow, or any other bright color. The knitted pattern will show up just as well and you will have an updated classic that goes with everything.

You can use any type of yarn you wish, but I suggest using some type of acrylic since they are machine-washable. Experiment with yarns as you would with fabric.

KNITTING ABBREVIATIONS

k–knit
p–purl
st(s)–stitch(es)
St st–Stockinette stitch
sk–skip
sl–slip
pat–pattern
beg–begin(ning)
rep–repeat
dec–decrease
inc–increase
rem–remain(ing)
SKP–slip 1 st, k next st, pass slip st over knit st
tog–together
psso–pass slip stitch over

FLAT KNIT TURTLENECK OR CREW NECK PULLOVER

Sizes: Directions are for Small (1–2). Changes for Medium (3–4) and Large (5–6) are in parentheses.

Materials: Sport-Weight 2-Ply (2 oz. skeins)
 Solid: 4 skeins
 Stripe Pat # 1: 2 each colors A & B
 Stripe Pat # 2: 2 color A, 1 each B, C, & D
 Stripe Pat # 3: 1 each colors A, B, C, D, E, F, G, H, I, J, K, & L
Knitting Needles Nos. 5 & 6 or size to give gauge.

Gauge: 5 sts to 1″; 7 rows to 1″

Finished Measurement: Chest: 23 (25–27)″

Stripe Pat # 1 (2-color stripe): 4 rows each A & B
Stripe Pat # 2 (4-color stripe): * 2 rows B, 1 row C, 2 rows B, 8 rows D, 2 rows B, 1 row C, 2 rows B, 8 rows A. Repeat these 26 rows for stripes.
Stripe Pat # 3 (multicolor stripe) 4 rows each A, * B, C, D, E, F, G, H, I, J, K, & L, rep from * to end of piece.

Back: Beg at lower edge with No. 5 needles & A, cast on 54 (58–62) sts. Beg on wrong side work in k 1, p 1 rib for 1″ inc'ing 4 (4–5) sts evenly on last row—58 (62–67) sts. Change to No. 6 needles. Work in St st (k 1 row, p 1 row) and beg working in solid or stripe pat 1, 2, or 3 until 9½ (10–10½)″ from beg or desired length to underarm, end on right side.

Shape Raglan Armholes: Bind off 2 sts at beg of next 2 rows. *DEC ROW:* K 1, SKP, k to within last 3 sts, k 2 tog, k 1. Rep Dec Row every other row until 22 (24–27) sts rem. Slip to a holder.

Front: Work same as for Back until 34 (34–37) sts rem in raglan armhole, end on the right side.

Shape Neck (left side): P 11 (10–10) sts, slip to holder, p next 12 (14–17) sts, sl to holder, p rem sts. At neck edge bind off 2 sts twice, *and at the same time,* dec at armhole until 2 sts rem. *Next Row:* P 2 sts. *Next Row:* K 2 tog. Fasten off. *RIGHT SIDE:*

With right side facing you and keeping to pat, join yarn at neck edge, work to correspond to left side reversing all shaping.

Sleeves: Beg at lower edge with No. 5 needles and A, cast on 24 (26–28) sts. Beg on wrong side work in k 1, p 1 rib for 1½", inc'ing 9 sts on last row—33 (35–37) sts. Change to No. 6 needles. Beg working in solid or stripe pat same as for Back inc'ing 1 st at each end every 8th row 4 times. Work on 41 (43–45) sts until 10 (10½–11)" from beg or desired length to underarm, ending with same stripe as for Back.

Shape Raglan Armhole: Bind off 2 sts at beg of next 2 rows. Rep Dec Row same as for Back every other row until 5 sts rem. Slip rem sts to holder.

Finishing: Leaving right back raglan armhole open sew sleeves to Front and Back armholes.

Crew Neckband: With right side facing you, A and No. 6 needles, pick up and k 68 (68–74) sts around neck (including sts on holders). Work in k 1, p 1 rib for 1". Bind off loosely in rib. Sew open armhole including neckband.

Turtleneck: Work same as for Crew neck working in rib until 4" instead of 1". Bind off loosely in rib. Sew up armhole including 2" of turtleneck. Sew rem rows on right side. Sew side and sleeve seams.

Block

FISHERMAN'S KNIT TURTLENECK SWEATER & HAT

Sizes: Directions are for Small (1–2). Changes for Medium (3–4) and Large (5–6) are in parentheses.

Materials: Knitting Worsted Weight 4-Ply, 8 (10–12) ozs. Knitting Needles No. 8 or size to give gauge. 1 Cable Holder.

Gauge: 9 sts to 2"; 6 rows to 1".

Finished Measurement: *Chest:* 23 (25–27)"

Pullover

Back: Beg at lower edge, cast on 51 (55–61) sts.
Row 1: P 1, * k 1, p 1, rep from * across.
Row 2: K 1, * p 1, k 1, rep from * across.
REPEAT Rows 1 & 2 for rib for 2 (2–2½)", end with Row 1.
FOR SIZES SMALL & MEDIUM ONLY: Inc 1 st on last row.
FOR ALL SIZES—Row 1 (right side): P 6 (8–1) sts, place marker, sl next st, k next st *do not* sl off needle, k the sl st, sl both sts off left-hand needle *(rope made)*, [p 3, k 2, p 3, in next st k in front and back twice, then k in front *(5 sts in 1 st—beg of puff)*, p 3, k 2, p 3, work rope] 2 (2–3) times, place marker, p rem 6 (8–1) sts.
Row 2: K 6 (8–1) sts, sl marker, p 2, * k 3, p 2, k 11, p 2, k 3, p 2, rep from * to marker, sl marker, k last 6 (8–1) sts. *NOTE:* Always slip markers each row. Keeping sts outside markers in Reverse St st (k on wrong side, p on right side) work sts between markers as follows: *Row 3:* Work rope, [p 3, k 2, p 3, p 5 tog *(puff made)*, p 3, k 2, p 3, work rope] 2 (2–3) times, p rem sts. *Row 4:* P 2, * k 3, p 2, k 7, p 2, k 3, p 2, rep from * to marker. *Row 5:* Work rope, * p 3, sl next 2 sts onto cable holder and hold in front of work, p next st, k 2 sts from holder *(left twist—LT)*, p 5, sl next st onto cable holder and hold in back of work, k next 2 sts, p st from holder *(right twist—RT)*, p 3, work rope, rep from * to marker. *Row 6:* P 2, * k 4, p 2, k 5, p 2, k 4, p 2, rep from * to marker. *Row 7:* Work rope, * p 4, LT, p 3, RT, p 4, work rope, rep from * to marker. *Row 8:* P 2, * k 5, p 2, k 3, p 2, k 5, p 2, rep from * to marker. *Row 9:* Work rope, * p 2, beg puff, p 2, LT, p 1 RT, p 2, beg puff, p 2, work rope, rep from * to marker. *Row 10:* P 2, * k 10, p 2, k 1, p 2, k 10, p 2, rep from * to marker. *Row 11:* Work rope, * p 2, p 5 tog, p 3, k 2, p 1, k 2, p 3, p 5 tog, p 2, work rope, rep from * to marker. *Row 12:* P 2, * k 6, p 2, k 1, p 2, k 6, p 2, rep from * to marker. *Row 13:* Work rope, * p 5, RT, p 1, LT, p 5, work rope, rep from * to marker. *Row 14:* Rep Row 8. *Row 15:* Work rope, * p 4, RT, p 3, LT, p 4, work rope, rep from * to marker. *Row 16:* P 2, * k 4, p 2, k 5, p 2, k 4, p 2, rep from * to marker. *Row 17:* Work rope, * p 3, RT, p 2, beg puff, p 2, LT, p 3, work rope, rep from * to marker. *Row 18:* Rep Row 2. Last 16

rows form pat. Work in pat until 9½ (10½–11½)″ from beg or desired length to underarm, end on the wrong side. *NOTE:* If puff st or rope falls close to shaping edge work in Reverse St st. Count 5 sts of each puff as 1 st.

Shape Armhole: Keeping to pat bind off 3 (3–4) sts at beg of next 2 rows. Dec 1 st at each end every other row 3 times. Work in pat as established on 40 (44–47) sts until armholes measure 4 (4½–5)″, end on the wrong side.

Shape Shoulder: Bind off 4 sts at beg of next 4 rows, then bind off 4 (5–5) sts at beg of next 2 rows. Place rem 16 (18–21) sts on holder for neck.

Front: Work same as for Back until armholes measure 2¼ (2¾–3)″, end on the wrong side.
SHAPE NECK: Row 1 (left side): Work in pat across 15 (16–16) sts, place rem sts on holder. Keeping to pat dec 1 st at neck every other row 3 times. Work in pat as established on 12 (13–13) sts until armhole measures same as Back to shoulder, end at armhole edge being sure to end with same pat row as for Back.

Shape Shoulder: Row 1: Bind off 4 sts, work in pat across. *Row 2:* Work in pat across. *Rows 3 & 4:* Rep Rows 1 & 2 of shoulder. Bind off remaining sts. *RIGHT SIDE:* With right side facing you, slip next 10 (12–15) sts to holder, sl rem 15 (16–16) sts onto needle. Beg at neck work to correspond to left side reversing all shaping.

Sleeves: Beg at lower edge, cast on 26 (26–28) sts. Work in k 1, p 1 rib for 2 (2–2½)″. inc'ing 5 sts evenly across last row, 31 (31–33) sts. Work in pat as follows: *Row 1:* P 5 (5–6) sts, place marker, work rope, p 3, k 2, p 3, beg puff, p 3, k 2, p 3, work rope, place marker, p 5 (5–6) sts. *Row 2:* K 5 (5–6) sts, sl marker, p 2, k 3, p 2, k 11, p 2, k 3, p 2, sl marker, k rem sts. Beg with Row 3 of pat for Back work same as for Back omitting rep and inc'ing 1 st at each end every 7th row 4 (6–7) times.
NOTE: Work inc sts in Reverse St st. Work in pat as established on 39 (43–47) sts until 9½ (10½–11½)″ from beg, end on the wrong side.
SHAPE CAP: Bind off 3 (3–4) sts at beg on next 2 rows. Dec 1 st at each end of every other row 4 (6–7) times, then rep dec every row 8 times. Bind off rem 9 sts.

Finishing: Sew right shoulder together.
Turtleneck: With right side facing you pick up and k 62 (66–72) sts around neck (including sts on holders). Work in k 1, p 1 rib for 4 (4–4½)″. Bind off loosely in rib. Sew left shoulder and turtleneck. Sew sleeve seams. Sew in sleeves.

Block

Fisherman's Hat

Sizes: Directions are for Small. Changes for Medium are in parentheses.

Materials: Knitting Worsted Weight 4-Ply, 4 ozs. Knitting Needles No. 4 for Small, No. 6 for Medium.

Gauge: SMALL: 11 sts to 2″; 15 rows to 2″.
Gauge: MEDIUM: 5 sts to 1″; 7 rows to 1″.

Finished Measurements: Small—18″; Medium —19″.

NOTE: See Fisherman knit sweater for how to work special stitches.

Hat

Beg at cuff with No. 4 (6) needles, cast on 96 sts. Work in k 1, p 1 rib for 2 (2½)″. *Row 1 (right side):* P 2, * work rope, p 3, k 2, p 3, beg puff, p 3, k 2, p 3, rep from * across, end p 2 instead of p 3. *Row 2:* K 2, * p 2, k 11, (p 2, k 3) twice, rep from * across, end p 2, k 3, p 2, k 2 instead of (p 2, k 3) twice. *Row 3:* P 2, * work rope, p 3, k 2, p 3, p 5 tog (puff made), p 3, k 2, p 3, rep from * across, end p 2 instead of p 3. *Row 4:* K 2, * p 2, k 7, (p 2, k 3) twice, rep from * across, end same as for Row 2. *Row 5:* P 2, * work rope, p 3, LT, p 5, RT, p 3, rep from * across, end p 2 instead of p 3. *Row 6:* K 3, * p 2, k 5, (p 2, k 4) twice, rep from * across, end k 2 instead of k 4. *Row 7:* P 2, * work rope, p 4, LT, p 3, RT, p 4, rep from * across, end p 3 instead of p 4. *Row 8:* K 4, * p 2, k 3, (p 2, k 5) twice, rep from * across, end k 2 instead of k 5. *Row 9:* P 2, * work rope, p 2, beg puff, p 2, LT, p 1, RT, p 2, beg puff, p 2, rep from * across, end p 1 instead of p 2. *Row 10:* K 9, * p 2, k 1, (p 2, k 10) twice, rep from * across, end p 2, k 10, p 2, k 2 instead of (p 2, k 10) twice. *Row 11:* P 2, * work rope, p 2, p 5 tog, p 3, k 2, p 1, k 2, p 3, p 5 tog, p 2, rep from * across, end p 1 instead of p 2. *Row 12:* K 5, * p 2, k 1, (p 2, k 6)

53

twice, rep from * across, end k 2 instead of k 6. *Row 13:* P 2, * work rope, p 5, RT, p 1, LT, p 5, rep from * across, end p 4 instead of p 5. *Row 14:* Rep Row 8. *Row 15:* P 2, * work rope, p 4, RT, p 3, LT, p 4, rep from * across, end with p 3 instead of p 4. *Row 16:* Rep Row 6. *Row 17:* P 2, * work rope, p 3, RT, p 2, beg puff, p 2, LT, p 3, rep from * across, end p 2 instead of p 3. *Row 18:* Rep Row 2. Rep Rows 3 through 18 once, then rep Rows 3 and 4 once.

SHAPE TOP: Row 1: P 2, * work rope, p 3, k 2, p 2 tog, p 3, p 2 tog, k 2, p 3, rep from * across, end p 2 instead of p 3 (86 sts). *Row 2:* K 2, * p 2, k 5 (p 2, k 3) twice, rep from * across, end k 2 instead of k 3. *Row 3:* P 2, * work rope, p 3, k 2, p 2 tog, p 1, p 2 tog, k 2, p 3, rep from * across, end p 2 instead of p 3 (76 sts). *Row 4:* K 2, * p 2, k 3, rep from * across, end k 2 instead of k 3. *Row 5:* P 2, * work rope, p 3, k 2, p 3 tog, k 2, p 3, rep from * across, end p 2 instead of p 3 (66 sts). *Row 6:* K 2, * p 2, k 1, (p 2, k 3) twice, rep from * across, end k 2 instead of k 3. *Row 7:* P 2, * work rope, p 3, k 1, sl 1, k 2 tog, psso, k 1, p 3, rep from * across, end p 2 instead of p 3

(56 sts). *Row 8:* K 2, * p 3, k 3, p 2, k 3, rep from * across, end k 2 instead of k 3. *Row 9:* P 2, * work rope, p 3, sl 1, k 2 tog, psso, p 3, rep from * across, end p 2 instead of p 3 (46 sts). *Row 10:* K 2, * p 1, k 3, p 2, k 3, rep from * across, end k 2 instead of k 3. *Row 11:* P 2, * k 2 tog, p 3 tog, k 1, p 3 tog, rep from * across, end p 2 tog instead of p 3 tog (22 sts). Break off, leaving a 12″ strand. Thread strand through rem sts and draw tightly. Fasten securely on wrong side. Beg at top sew back seam to within 1 (1½)″ from beg of rib. On right side sew rem of hat.

Pom Pom for Hat: Cut 2 cardboard circles 2″ in diameter. Cut hole 1¼″ in diameter in center. Cut 4 strands of yarn 8 yards long. With circles tog wind yarn around drawing yarn through center opening and over edge until center hole is filled. Cut yarn around outer edge between circles. Double ½ yard length of yarn. Slip between 2 cardboard circles and tie securely around strands of pom pom. Remove cardboard and trim evenly. Sew to top of hat.

Flat knit pullover: Close-up of 3-color stripe

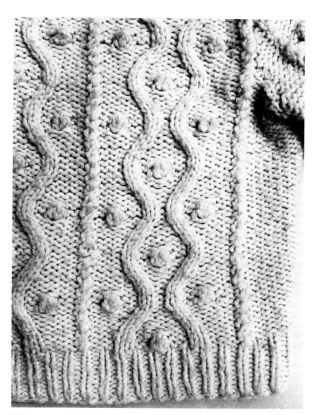

Fisherman's knit sweater: Close-up of pattern

The
Decorations

DECORATING THE GARMENT

In most cases a garment should be decorated before the pieces are sewn together. It's much easier to work on flat pieces and your work will be much neater. Mark center front guide lines with a basting thread. Each technique for decorating, appliqué, embroidery, and pockets, is given in a separate section, but they can be combined. Take ideas from each section and incorporate them on one garment.

Appliqué

Appliqué is the technique of applying one piece of fabric to another. The appliqué pattern can be very simple or quite intricate. For example, one simple flower can be cut out of one piece of fabric and applied to the garment, or a flower can be cut with stem, petals, leaves, and shading, each piece of the flower cut from a different fabric. Fabrics with different prints, textures, and colors can be combined. When choosing fabrics for appliqué, make sure they are colorfast and preshrunk if the garment will be washed. If you plan to dry-clean only, you can use anything. The following decorations were designed for the garments in this book, but they can also be applied to any garment using the same basic techniques.

SUPPLIES FOR APPLIQUÉ

1. *Fabric* or fabric scraps
2. 1″ or 2″ plastic see-through *ruler*
3. *Sharp needles, thread,* and *thimble*
4. *Lightweight cardboard* (manila folders, 8½″ by 11″)
5. *Pencils, pen,* and *tracing paper* (8½″ by 11″)
6. *Small sharp scissors*
7. *Steam iron* and *ironing board*

HOW TO APPLIQUÉ

1. First, trace the pattern from the book onto a piece of tracing paper. (Each pattern is life-size.) Make sure you also trace the center line marked on the pattern. Once traced, turn the tracing paper over and using back-and-forth strokes, darken the back of the traced lines with a soft lead pencil. Right side up, place the tracing on lightweight cardboard (manila folders work well for this) and re-draw the original traced lines with a soft pencil, pressing firmly. The soft leaded back will act as a carbon and will transfer the image. Draw over your lines on the cardboard to make them permanent.

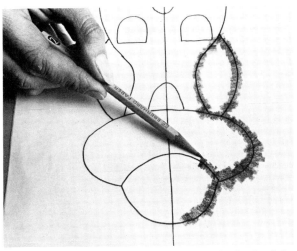

Turn the tracing paper over and darken the back of the traced lines with a soft lead pencil.

Place the tracing on cardboard, right side up, and re-draw the original traced lines, pressing firmly. The soft-leaded back will act as a carbon and transfer the image.

2. You may want to embroider a piece such as the ribbon or scroll before it is appliquéd. Trace the pattern onto tracing paper and fill name or initials between the dotted lines. In order to center the letters, trace them first onto a separate piece of paper and then find the center by dividing the name in two with a vertical dotted line. Place the letters under the traced pattern, align the dotted lines, and copy them. Now transfer your letters to the fabric (See "Embroidery," page 81) and embroider. (Make sure the fabric is cut large enough to fit into an embroidery hoop.) Now you can cut out the appliqué and apply it to the garment, adding any further embroidery details once it's on the garment.

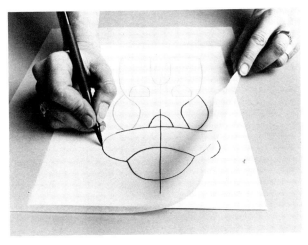

First trace the pattern from the book onto a piece of tracing paper.

59

When embroidering on appliqué, trace the appliqué pattern onto tracing paper, then fill in name or initials between the dotted lines.

3. Cut out the entire cardboard pattern and position it on the garment, matching the center lines if it goes on the front. Make sure it is not too close to any edge of the garment, allowing 1″ from a seamline. This is so you do not lose any of the appliqué when your seams are sewn together.

Cut out the cardboard pattern and position it on the garment.

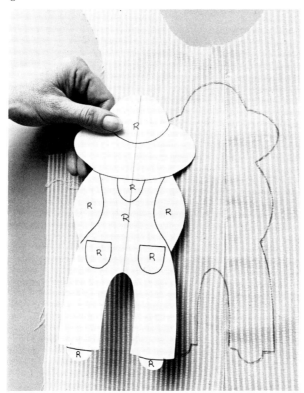

Once you have placed the pattern, trace around it on the garment with chalk or a very fine-line pencil. Use something that will not leave a permanent heavy line. Now you have guide lines to follow when you sew the appliqué to the garment.

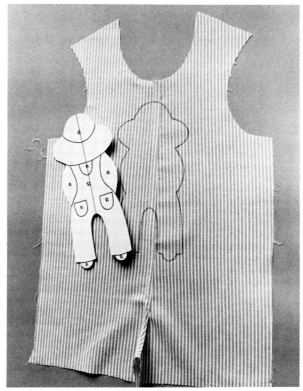

Trace around it with chalk or a fine-line pencil.

4. Mark each piece of your cardboard pattern with an "R" on the right side and then cut up the pieces. Place each pattern piece on the *wrong* side

Cut out the pattern pieces, place each piece on the wrong side of the fabric and trace.

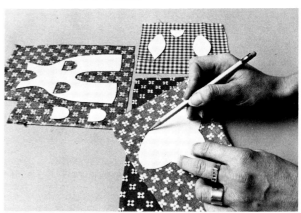

60

of the side of the fabrics you have chosen for the appliqué and trace around them. (Put the *right* side of your pattern down on the *wrong* side of the fabric.) Allow ¼″ seam allowance around each piece and cut them out. If there are any curves, clip around the edge so the seam lies flat when it is turned.

Cut the pieces, and clip any curves.

5. Place the cardboard pattern piece on the wrong side of the cut piece and press in the edges with an iron. Do this with each piece. This guarantees neatly turned-in edges and an accurate copy of your pattern piece.

Place the cardboard pattern on the wrong side of the cut piece and press in the edges with an iron.

6. Arrange the pieces on the garment using the original outline as your guide line. Baste or pin the pieces on, making sure the turned-in edges are neat and flat.

Arrange the pieces on the garment and pin or baste them in place.

7. If you are doing a patchwork appliqué such as the star, tree, or the patchwork letters, sew the pieces together first and then apply them to the garment. Stitch the pieces together by machine or

If you are doing patchwork appliqué, sew the pieces together first, and then apply the entire design to the garment.

Stitch the design to the garment by hand.

You may find designs already printed on fabric that work well as appliqué. Use the same method for applying them to the garment.

hand following the ¼″ seam allowance accurately. Press in the outside edges and apply the complete appliqué to the garment using a single thread and small hemming stitches.

8. Sometimes you may find a motif already printed on a piece of fabric that would make a nice appliqué. Cut out the motif allowing ¼″ seam allowance all around and clip the curves. Turn in the edges and baste or pin to the garment. Using a single thread and small hemming stitches, apply the appliqué to the garment. (You can also attach it by machine, using a zig zag stitch close together.) When the appliqué is completed, sew the entire garment together.

9. Sew the pieces on using small hemming stitches with matching thread for each piece. They should be neat, even, small stitches so they do not show and will wear well. Once the hem stitch has been completed, take out all the basting and press the entire appliqué so it is flat.

10. If you wish to do any embroidery on the appliqué, trim it so that it fits into an embroidery hoop. Using a marking pencil, draw the design on the appliqué. Do not draw heavy lines unless you are sure the embroidery will cover them.

GENERAL INFORMATION ABOUT THESE APPLIQUÉ PATTERNS

1. The *heavy black line* is the outline for each pattern piece of the appliqué. Each piece can be cut in a different color or a fabric pattern. Use as many colors or fabrics as you wish for each appliqué design.

2. The *fine lines* on the appliqué patterns represent embroidery stitches that can be added after the appliqué has been applied. The embroidery stitches have been suggested but you can use any you think will work. Use 6-strand embroidery floss, or separate it for finer lines. Use as many colors as you wish for the embroidery.

3. The *vertical dotted line* on each pattern is a guide for centering the appliqué, if you wish. Use this line also as a straight grain line. Lines with double pointed arrows mark any grain line other than the dotted line.

4. For names or initials, take the letters from the alphabets in the embroidery section.

5. These patterns are the actual size you will use on a child's clothes. Simply trace the pattern right from the book.

Rows of stem stitch for rainbow

Rows of stem stitch for sun,
backstitch for rays

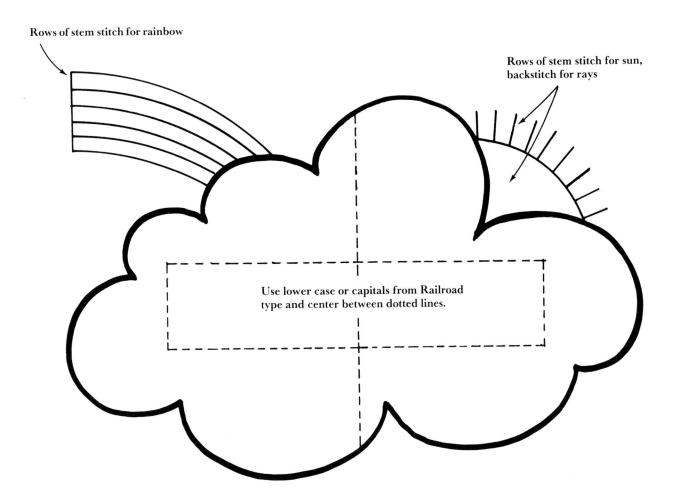

Use lower case or capitals from Railroad
type and center between dotted lines.

Note: Embroider name on first, apply cloud to garment, then
add sun and rainbow embroidery stitches.

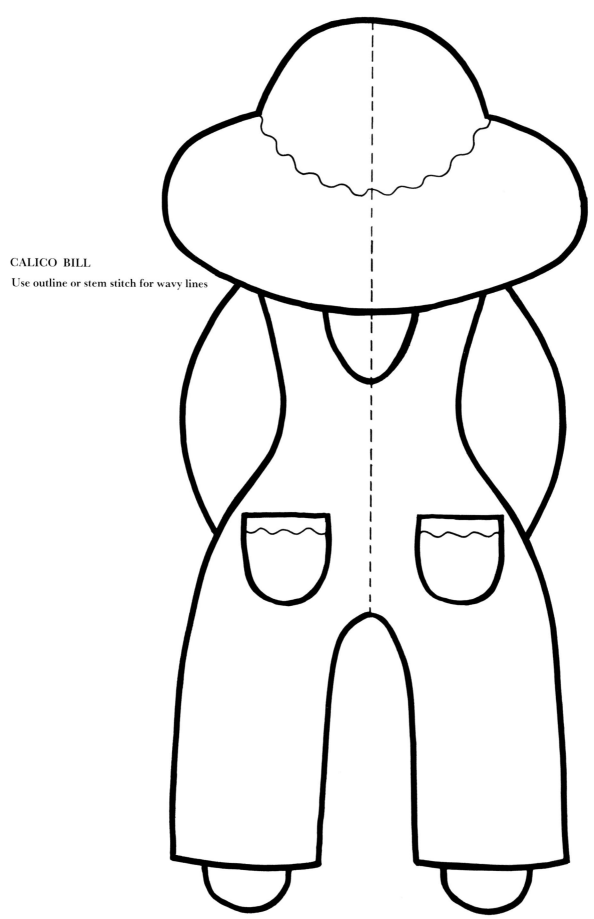

CALICO BILL

Use outline or stem stitch for wavy lines

64

*Two styles made from the jacket pattern: A tunic dress with patch block
pockets, and a blue denim painting smock with a jean-style pouch pocket.*

*The button-shoulder dress has a pouch pocket embroidered with
the "Strawberries" and "Wildflowers" patterns. The bibbed
overalls are decorated with the embroidered "Vegetables." On both
styles, the names are embroidered with the Railroad alphabet.*

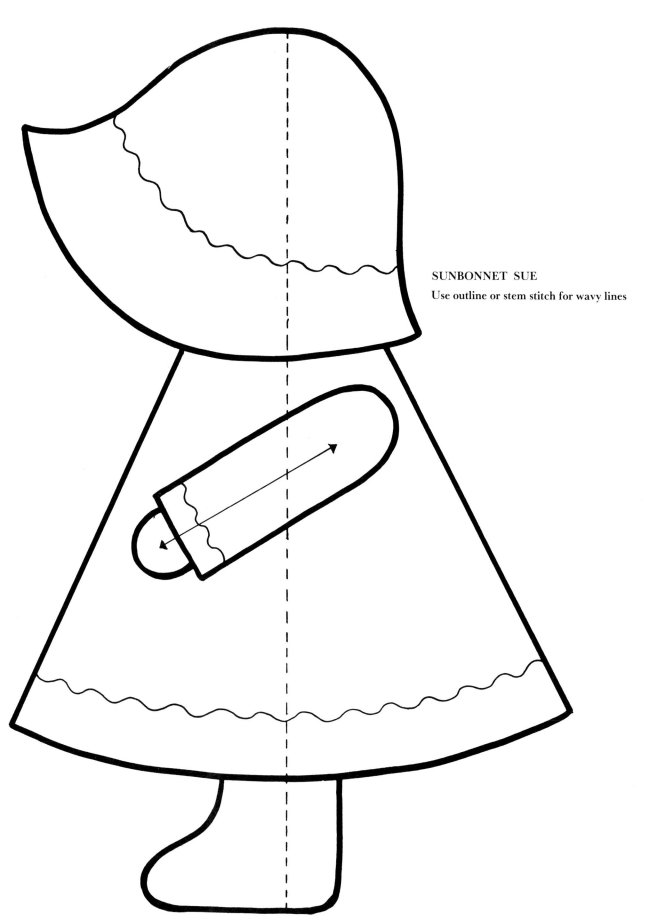

SUNBONNET SUE

Use outline or stem stitch for wavy lines

Running stitch for veins on leaves

Embroider leaves after the appliqué has been applied.

NOTE: Apply apple, stem, and then leaves.

APPLE

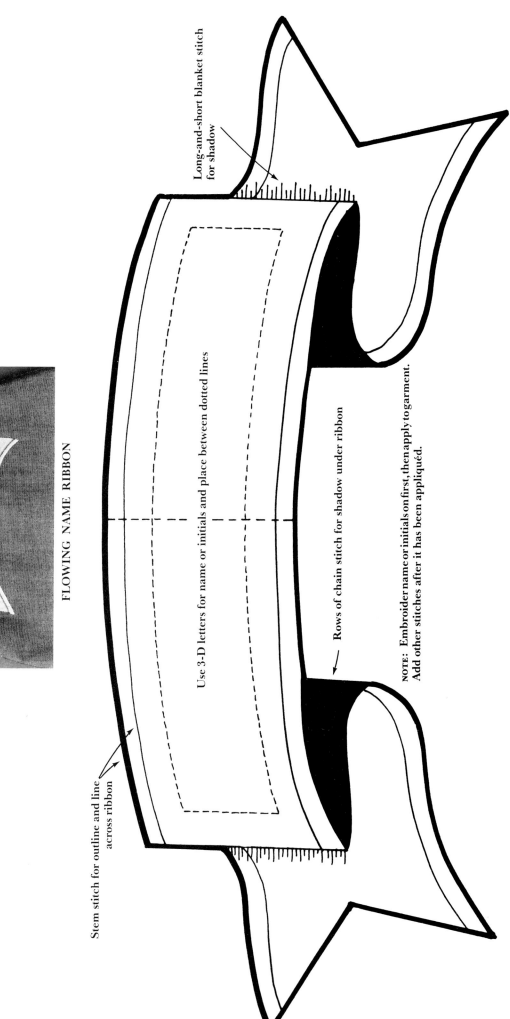

FLOWING NAME RIBBON

Long-and-short blanket stitch for shadow

Use 3-D letters for name or initials and place between dotted lines

Rows of chain stitch for shadow under ribbon

NOTE: Embroider name or initials on first, then apply to garment. Add other stitches after it has been appliquéd.

Stem stitch for outline and line across ribbon

PATCHWORK HOUSE

NOTE: Join house, roof and chimneys together. Cut out windows and door and apply to house. Apply entire house to garment.

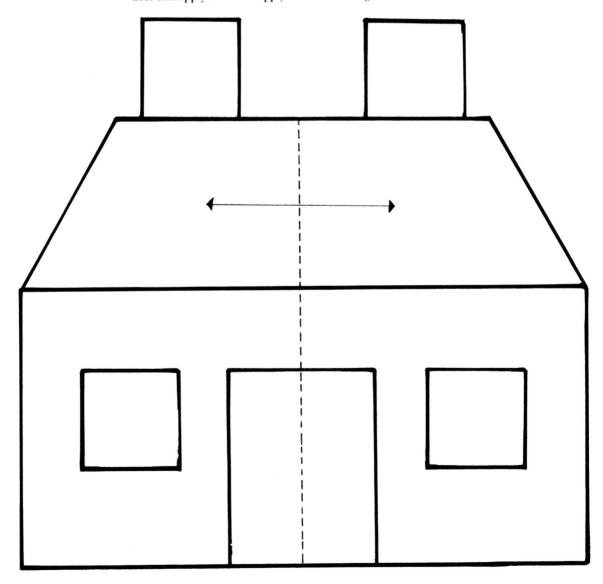

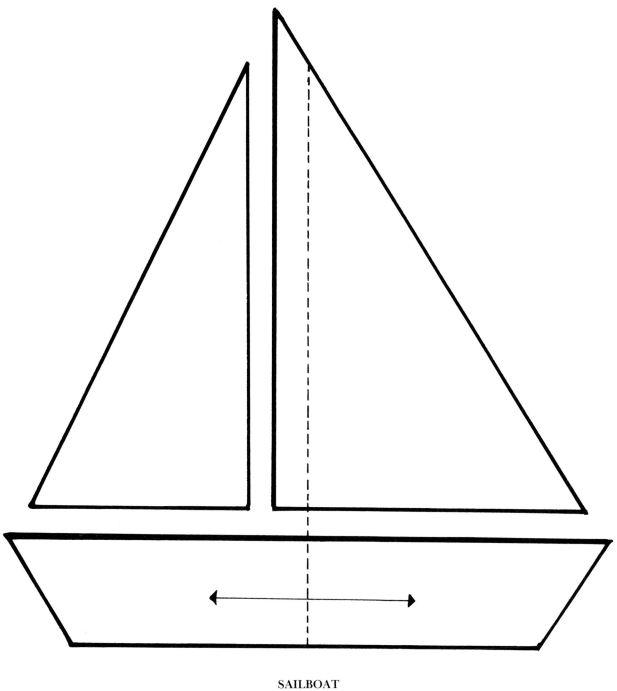

SAILBOAT

Note: Apply each piece to garment. You could embroider an initial on the large sail.

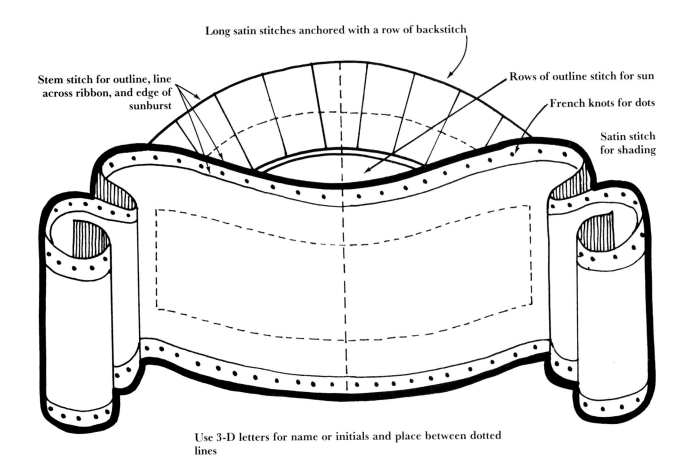

Long satin stitches anchored with a row of backstitch

Stem stitch for outline, line across ribbon, and edge of sunburst

Rows of outline stitch for sun

French knots for dots

Satin stitch for shading

Use 3-D letters for name or initials and place between dotted lines

NOTE: Embroider name on first, then apply scroll to garment. Add sunburst and other embroidery stitches after the appliqué is on the garment.

NAME SCROLL WITH EMBROIDERED SUNBURST

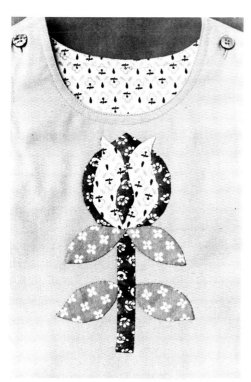

PATCHWORK FLOWER

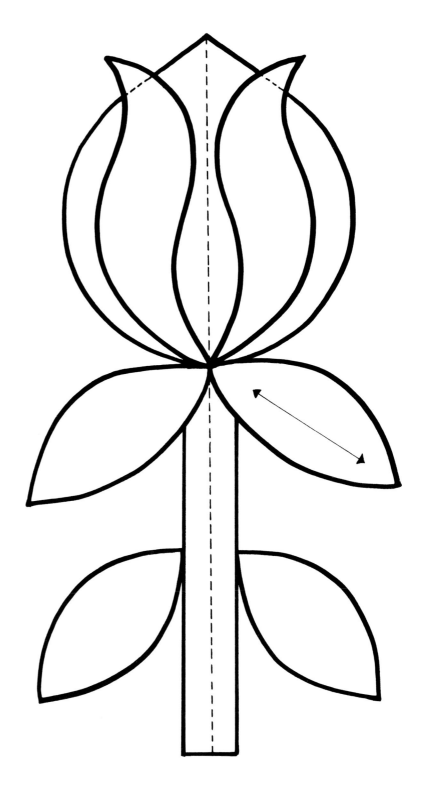

NOTE: Apply stem and base flower first, then apply leaves and flower petals

71

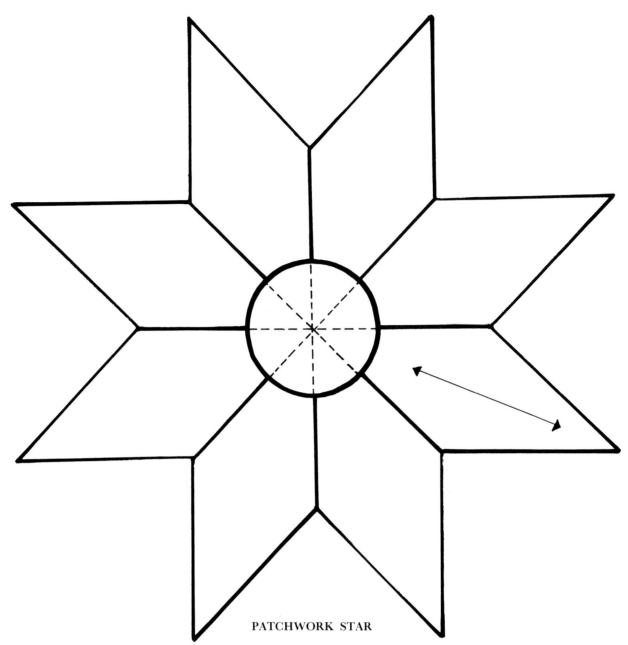

PATCHWORK STAR

NOTE: Cut out pieces of star and join together, then apply to garment. If you want the circle in the center, appliqué it over the star.

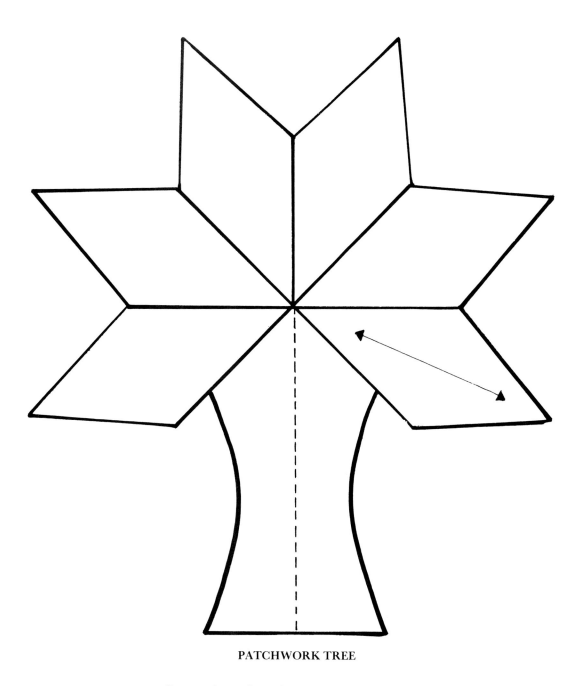

PATCHWORK TREE

NOTE: Cut out pieces of tree, join together, then apply to garment.

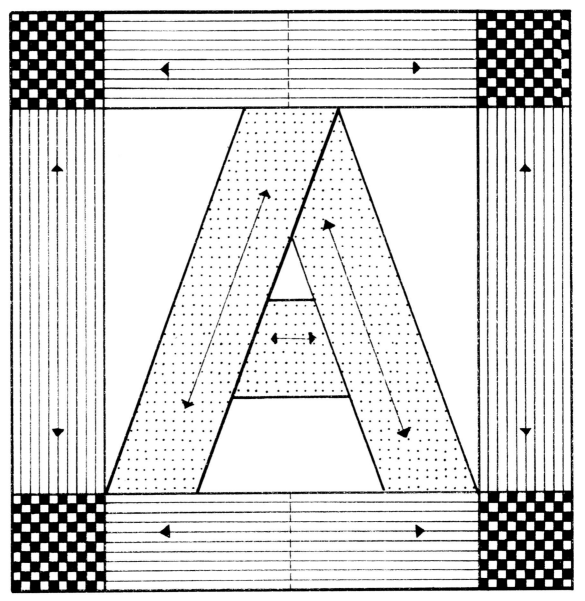

The straight grain lines have been suggested on the letter "A." Generally the grain line should run in the center of each piece of the letter. The background should have a vertical straight grain parallel to the center line.

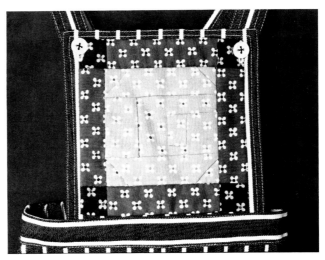

PATCHWORK INITIALS

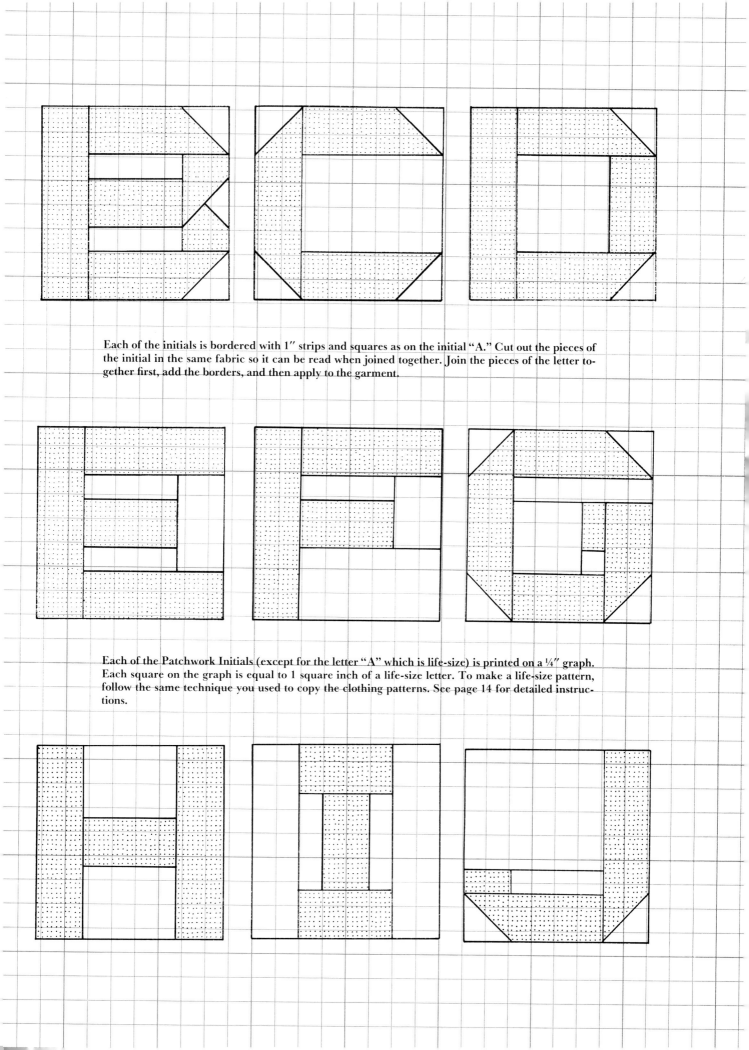

Each of the initials is bordered with 1″ strips and squares as on the initial "A." Cut out the pieces of the initial in the same fabric so it can be read when joined together. Join the pieces of the letter together first, add the borders, and then apply to the garment.

Each of the Patchwork Initials (except for the letter "A" which is life-size) is printed on a ¼″ graph. Each square on the graph is equal to 1 square inch of a life-size letter. To make a life-size pattern, follow the same technique you used to copy the clothing patterns. See page 14 for detailed instructions.

76

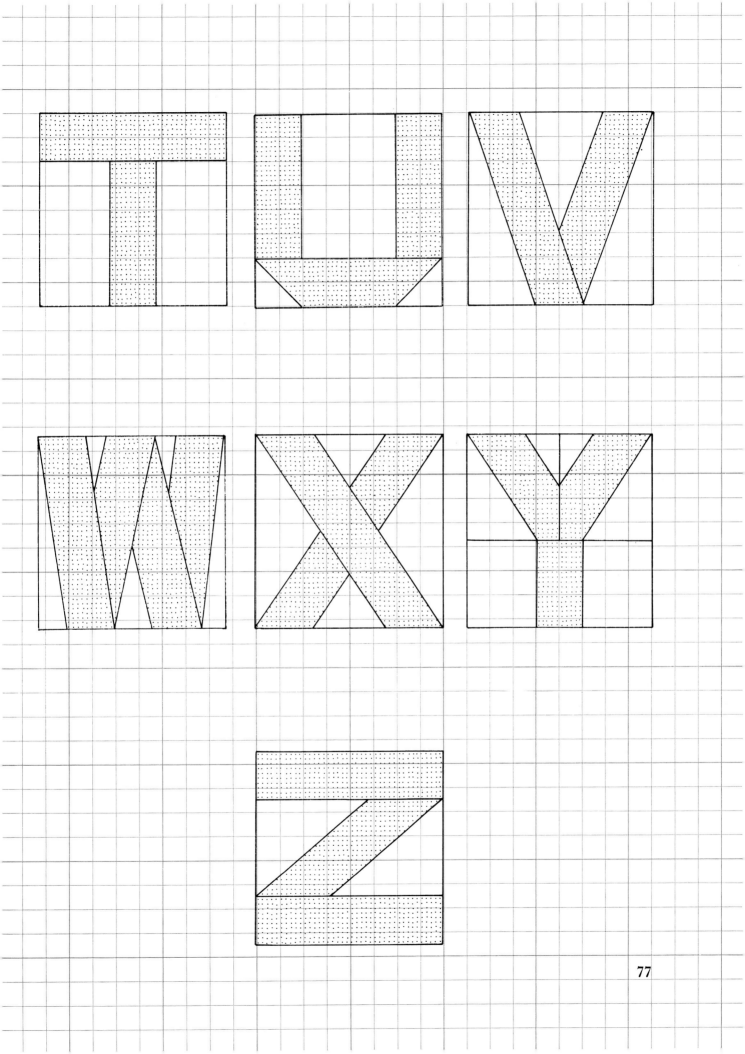

Embroidery

Embroidery designs can be as simple or as complicated as you wish and can be worked on almost any fabric. You can use very few stitches, or incorporate many stitches into a single design. You can use many kinds of thread or yarn, but I recommend 6-strand cotton embroidery floss because it's colorfast and washes beautifully. You can use all 6 strands or separate the threads for finer work. There is a tremendous color range available and it can be readily purchased at any dime store or yarn department. Other types of yarns and threads can be used, but make sure they are colorfast if the finished garment is to be washed.

79

The button-shoulder dress is appliquéd with the "Apple"
pattern. The button-shoulder jumpsuit has a zippered front and
flat patch pockets with flaps. The striped sweater was made
from the flat knit turtleneck pattern.

The boy's patchwork denim pants were made from the overall pattern, and the striped sweater was made from the flat knit turtleneck pattern. The girl's skirt is also made from the overalls pattern, and is embroidered with "The Patchwork Landscape" design.

The bibbed overalls are decorated with a "G" from the Monstre alphabet. The gray denim button-shoulder dress is decorated with the "Flowing Name Ribbon" appliqué.

Boy's and girl's bathrobe styles, both made from the jacket pattern.

You can embroider pieces of a garment before it is put together or add embroidery to a finished garment. For best results, use an embroidery hoop so that the fabric stays taut while you are working on it. If you want to embroider a small piece such as a pocket, cut your fabric large enough to fit in the hoop, do the embroidery, then cut out the pocket and apply it to the garment. If you are doing embroidery on a garment that is already put together, make sure that you don't sew the pieces together. (Don't embroider the pocket to the garment so that you can't then put your hand in.)

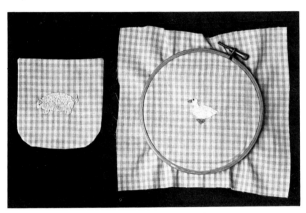

If embroidering a small piece, like a pocket, do the embroidery on a piece of fabric large enough to fit on a hoop, then cut out the pocket.

Once you have chosen your embroidery design, trace it onto a piece of tracing paper, marking the center guide line, if necessary. If there is a letter to be added, place the tracing paper over the letter, centering it in the space provided, and trace it. For a name or more than one letter, draw a straight line on the tracing paper, then place the

Center letters or a name in the space provided.

paper over and trace each letter. Watch the spacing between the letters so that it looks neat and even. If the name or initials is to be centered, divide the total measurement of the name in half and draw a vertical line. For example, if the name measures 5″ across, the vertical line would be drawn in the center, or 2½″ from each end. The vertical center line will be your guide line for placing it on the total design. You can do several tracings and combine them into one design. Using tracing paper, you can experiment with designs and try many different things.

Trace the design in pencil first, then darken the final line with black pen. Once your traced design is complete, transfer it to the fabric. Pin the tracing in place on the garment, slipping a piece of dressmaker's carbon between the paper and the fabric with the carbon side down. Outline the design carefully using a knitting needle or the back of a crochet hook. Press firmly when tracing so the design is visible.

Trace the design you have chosen on a piece of tracing paper, pin the paper on the garment, slip a carbon under, and transfer the design to the garment.

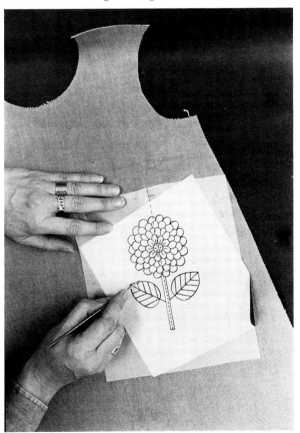

If the fabric is not too dark in color there is another way to transfer the design. Place the fabric over the design, pin it in place, and in daylight tape the fabric and design to the window. Trace the design directly on to the fabric with a regular pencil or a dressmaker's pencil, making sure the lines are not too heavy. A bright light bulb under a glass table or piece of glass will give the same results and make tracing easier because you'll be drawing on a flat surface.

You can also pin the tracing to the wrong side of the fabric, hold the garment up to a window, and transfer the pattern to the fabric directly.

Place the design in an embroidery hoop and stitch.

Once the design has been transferred to the fabric, place it in an embroidery hoop and begin stitching. If the entire design does not fit into the hoop, do the embroidery in sections.

SUPPLIES FOR EMBROIDERY

1. *Six-strand embroidery floss:* This is suggested for all the designs in this book, but you may use any thread or yarn you want.

2. *Embroidery or crewel needles* and a *thimble*

3. *Embroidery hoop,* 8″: You may use another size for larger or smaller designs, but this size will work for most designs in this book.

4. *Tracing paper,* 8½″ by 11″

5. *Dressmaker's carbon*

6. *A knitting needle, crochet hook,* or *tracing wheel* for tracing with carbon. A regular pencil or a dressmaker's pencil for tracing on fabric.

7. Small sharp pointed *scissors*

THE STITCHES

The stitches given here are basic. With each design I have suggested stitches and number of strands of floss to use, but experiment with your own ideas! Do not use bulky knots on embroidery. When starting or ending your thread, take one or two small backstitches on the wrong side of the fabric, trying not to go through to the right side.

The Outline Stitches: These are good stitches for lines and outlines. Rows of these stitches stitched close together can be used to cover areas. They can also be used as a base or foundation to cover with other stitches. The stitches should be done evenly so they look neat. They can be done in straight or curved lines.

1. *Outline* or *Stem stitch*. Work from left to right or top to bottom. Thread can be worked either side of needle, but once started keep it consistently above or below needle.

Outline or stem stitch

2. *Split stitch*. Work left to right same as outline stitch, but split the thread in the middle of the stitch when coming back instead of holding thread to one side.

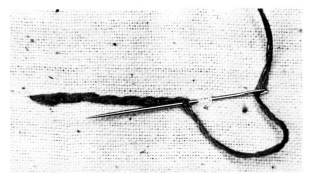

Split stitch

3. *Running stitch*. Work right to left, keeping stitches even. This is like a basting stitch.

Running stitch

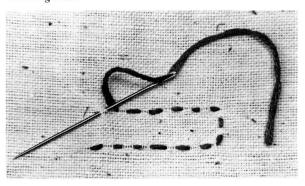

4. *Backstitch*. Work right to left or top to bottom and keep stitches even. This is good for outlines.

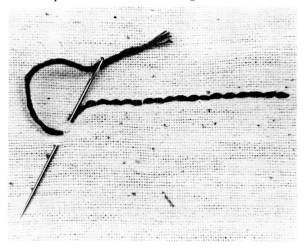

Backstitch

5. *Chain stitch*. Work right to left or top to bottom keeping stitches even in a chain.

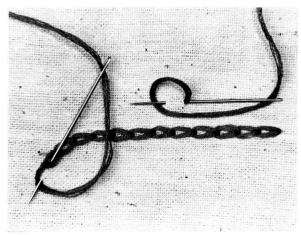

Chain stitch

The Cover Stitches: These stitches are used to fill in solid areas in the design.

1. *Satin stitch.* Straight stitches close together. They can go in any direction as long as they remain parallel and close together. This stitch is good for covering small areas.

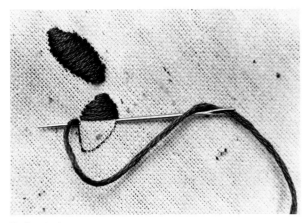

Satin stitch

2. *Padded Satin stitch.* First pad the area to be covered with outline, stem, or satin stitches close together. Cover the padded area with regular satin stitches, going in the opposite direction. This stitch works well for monograms.

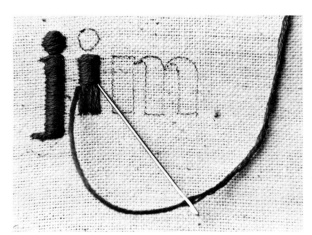

Padded satin stitch

Long & short stitch

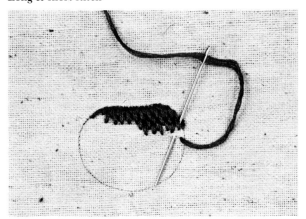

3. *Long & Short Satin stitches.* Work the same as the satin stitch except stagger long-and-short stitches over area to be covered. Keep stitches close together so that they cover.

Novelty Decorative Stitches: These are assorted stitches that can be incorporated in an embroidery pattern to give more variety.

1. *Lazy Daisy.* This is an individual chain stitch anchored at one end. Several done in a circle look like a daisy.

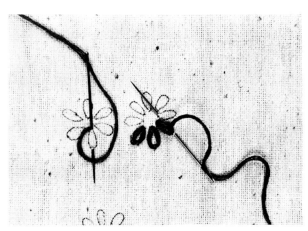

Lazy Daisy stitch

2. *Seed stitch.* These are tiny running stitches worked at random and scattered on an area. These are good to fill in an area that has been outlined.

Seed stitch

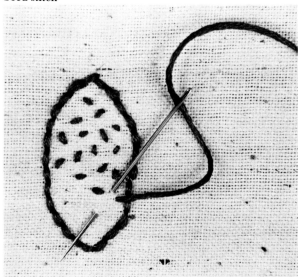

3. *French Knots.* These are very useful decorative spots. Done individually or in groups, they give texture to the embroidery.

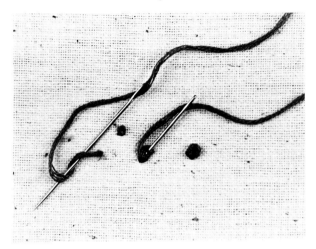

French knot

4. *Blanket* or *Buttonhole stitch.* Work from left to right and use them for edges, shadows, or finishing hand buttonholes. In the blanket stitch, the stitches are slightly apart; in the buttonhole stitch they are close together. The length of the stitch can be even for each stitch or staggered for a shaded effect.

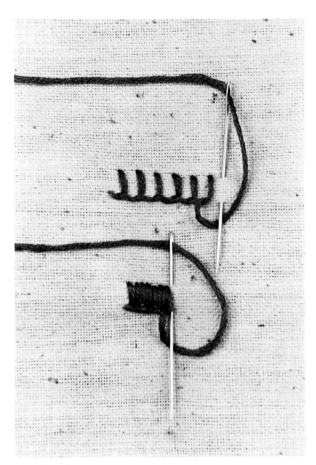

Blanket stitch, top; Buttonhole stitch, bottom

GENERAL INFORMATION ABOUT EMBROIDERY PATTERNS

1. The *vertical dotted line* is for centering the embroidery on the garment, if you wish.

2. Stitches and embroidery floss have been suggested for each design but can be changed in any way you may wish. You can also add or subtract stitches.

85

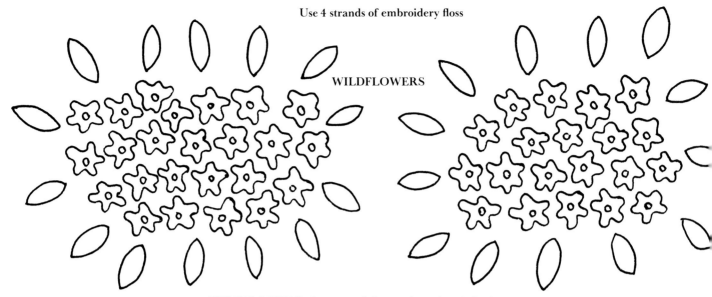

WILDFLOWERS

WILDFLOWERS: Leaves and flowers in satin stitch alternating 2 shades for flower and 2 greens for leaves. French knots in centers.

STRAWBERRIES

STRAWBERRIES: Fill in with satin stitch, black dots with French knots, stems and leaves outlined with stem stitch.

86

BARNYARD ANIMALS

Use 4 strands of embroidery floss, and fill in each animal with long-and-short satin stitches. Use satin stitch for the grass.

COW: Black and white or brown and white

LAMB: White with black

PIG: Pink with darker pink for shading, backstitch for tail, French knot for eye.

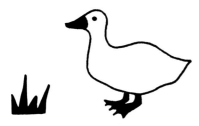

DUCK: White with orange bill and feet. French knot for eye.

Cow

Lamb

Pig

Duck

87

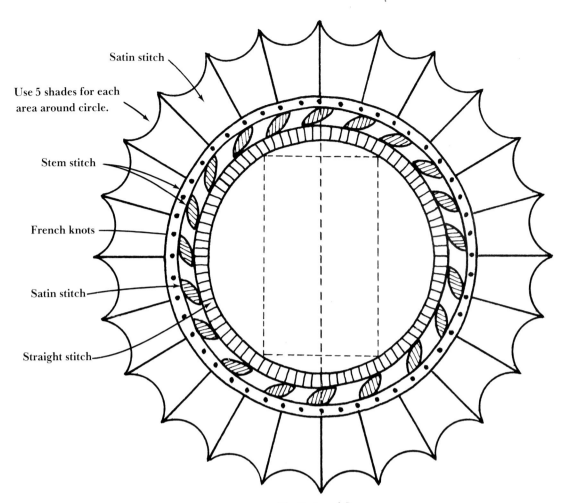

Satin stitch

Use 5 shades for each area around circle.

Stem stitch

French knots

Satin stitch

Straight stitch

Use 6-strand floss
Trace design and place Circus letter in center.

88

SUNBURST CIRCLE

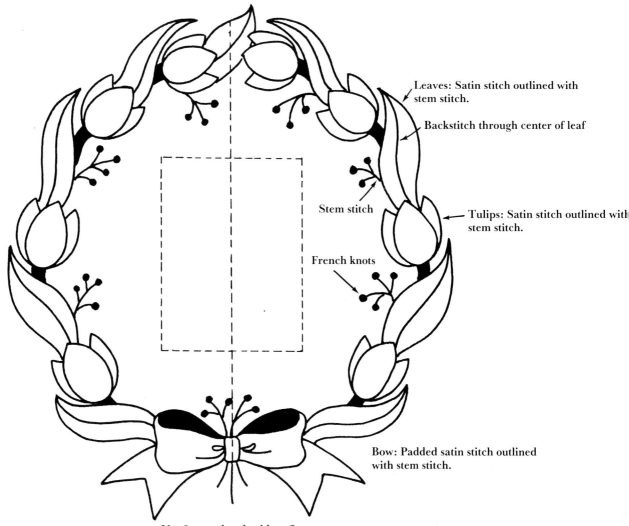

Leaves: Satin stitch outlined with stem stitch.

Backstitch through center of leaf

Stem stitch

Tulips: Satin stitch outlined with stem stitch.

French knots

Bow: Padded satin stitch outlined with stem stitch.

Use 6-strand embroidery floss
Trace design and place Circus letter in center.

CIRCLE OF TULIPS

89

Satin stitch with backstitch
through center of leaves

French knots

Use 3-D letters for initials

2 rows of chain stitch

OVAL WREATH

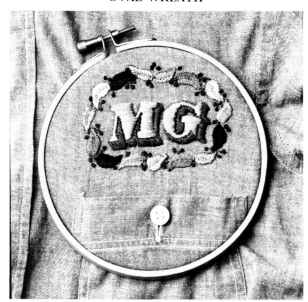

Outline stitch with
straight stitch in between

Clusters of French knots

Outline leaves only
with backstitch

Use Railroad letters for name

NAMEPLATE
Use 4 strands of embroidery floss

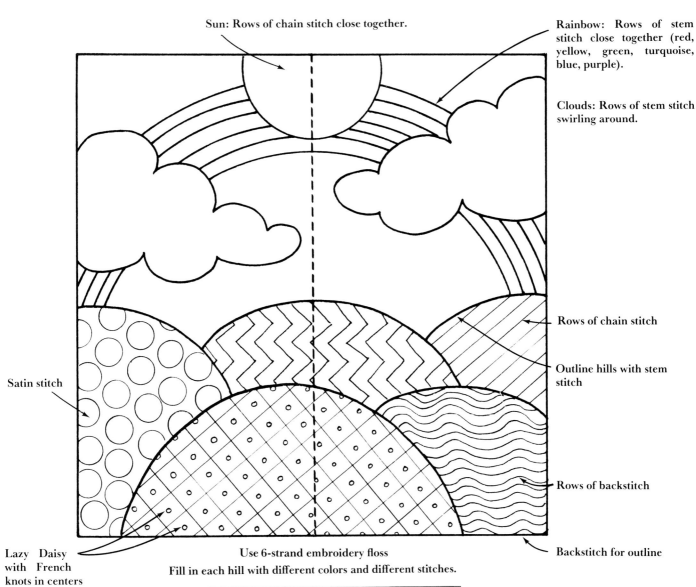

Sun: Rows of chain stitch close together.

Rainbow: Rows of stem stitch close together (red, yellow, green, turquoise, blue, purple).

Clouds: Rows of stem stitch swirling around.

Rows of chain stitch

Outline hills with stem stitch

Satin stitch

Rows of backstitch

Lazy Daisy with French knots in centers

Use 6-strand embroidery floss

Backstitch for outline

Fill in each hill with different colors and different stitches.

PATCHWORK SAMPLER

91

VEGETABLES
Use 4 strands of embroidery floss

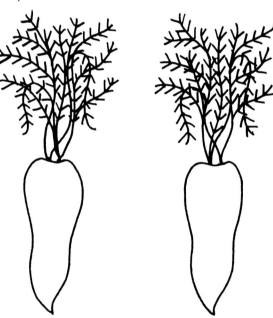

LETTUCE: Gold center—satin stitch. Leaves—buttonhole stitch (Use 3 or 4 shades of green)

CARROT: Fill in with long-and-short satin stitch, stems in stem stitch, leaves in straight stitch. Use 2 greens: 1 for stem, 1 for leaves.

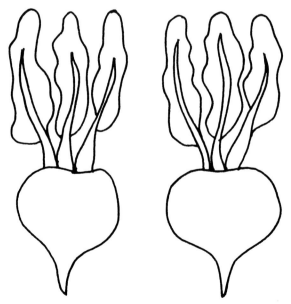

RADISH: Fill in with long-and-short satin stitches. Work leaves and centers in satin stitch using 2 or 3 greens.

TOMATO: Fill in with long-and-short satin stitches. Use 2 greens to work leaves in satin stitch.

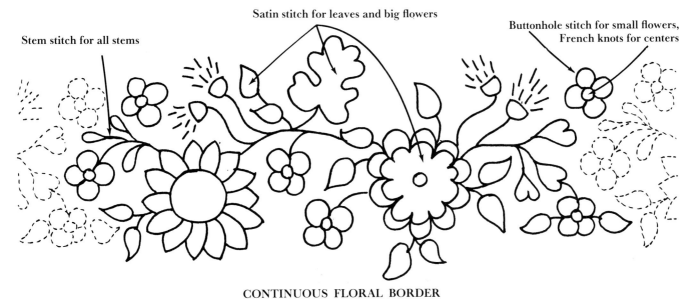

Stem stitch for all stems

Satin stitch for leaves and big flowers

Buttonhole stitch for small flowers, French knots for centers

CONTINUOUS FLORAL BORDER

NOTE: For a continuing floral border, trace motif and then trace again beside the first, tracing fitting in the flowers. (Dotted outlines are the same pattern repeated so you can see how it fits together.)

Make leaves and stems in shades of green and use as many colors as you wish for the flowers.

Padded satin

HEARTS: Embroider singly or repeat in continuous row.

POCKET MOTIF

Use 6-strand embroidery floss

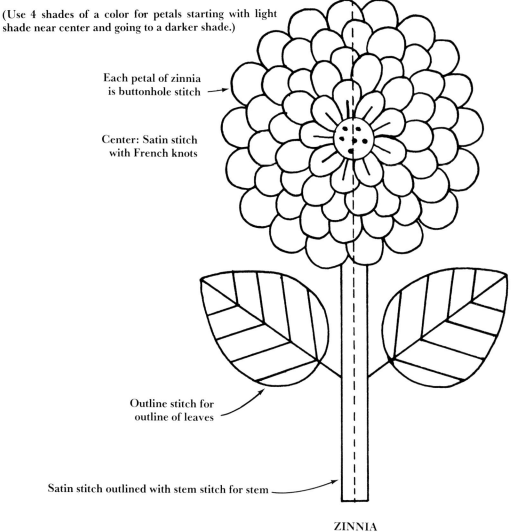

(Use 4 shades of a color for petals starting with light shade near center and going to a darker shade.)

Each petal of zinnia is buttonhole stitch →

Center: Satin stitch with French knots

Outline stitch for outline of leaves

Satin stitch outlined with stem stitch for stem

ZINNIA
Use 4 strands embroidery floss

MONSTRE ALPHABET

Treat each letter of the *Monstre Alphabet* as an embroidery sampler by trying different stitches and colors inside each letter.

For all of the letters, use 6-strand embroidery floss. Make the white outline with 2 rows of chain stitch close together.

Use padded satin stitch for shading with an outline stitch around the outside edge of the shadow.

To place a name inside the letter, trace the Monstre letter, then trace the name using the small linear alphabet. Place the Monstre letter over the traced name and mark it on the letter. Transfer the letter to the fabric.

94

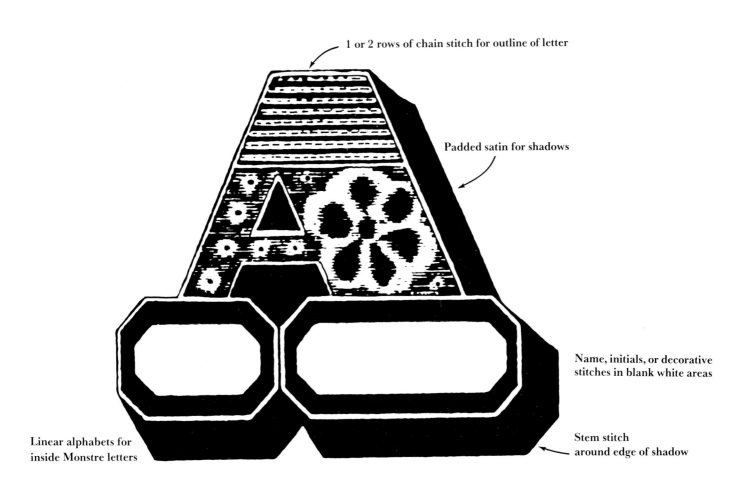

1 or 2 rows of chain stitch for outline of letter

Padded satin for shadows

Name, initials, or decorative stitches in blank white areas

Linear alphabets for inside Monstre letters

Stem stitch around edge of shadow

ABCDEFGHIJKLMNOPQRSTUVWXYZ&

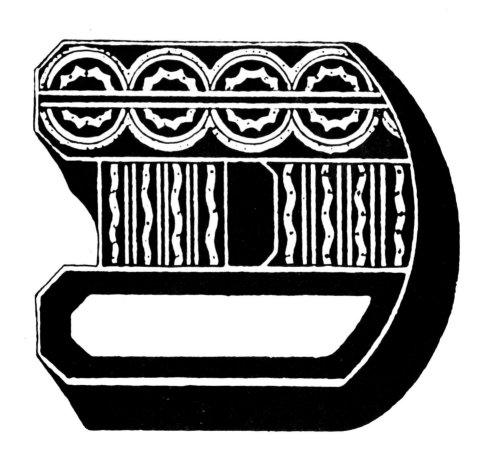

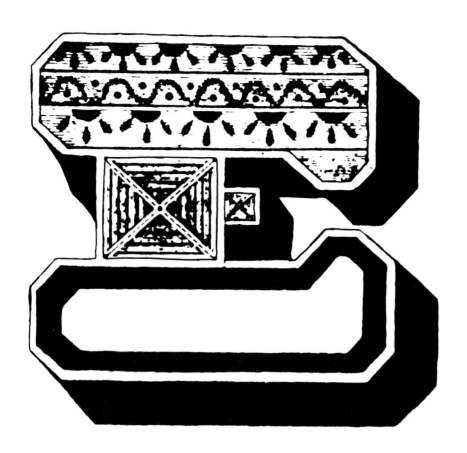

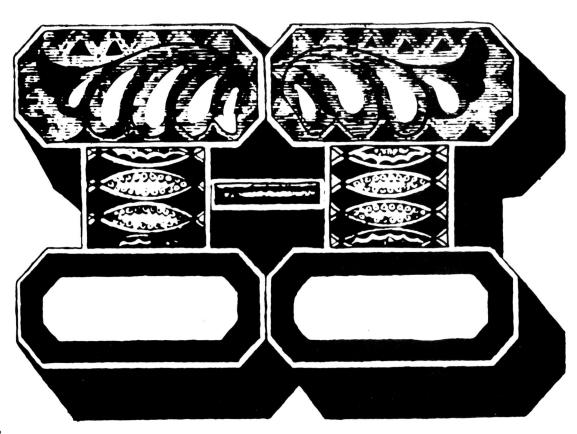

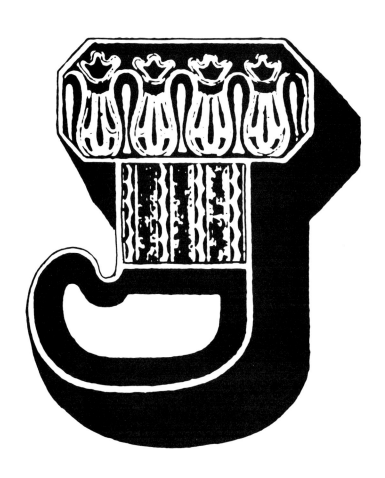

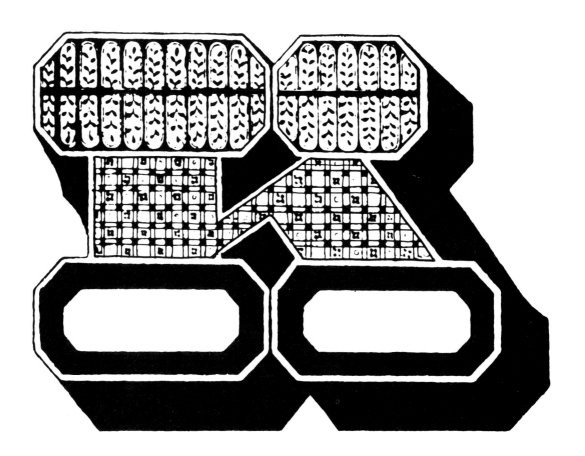

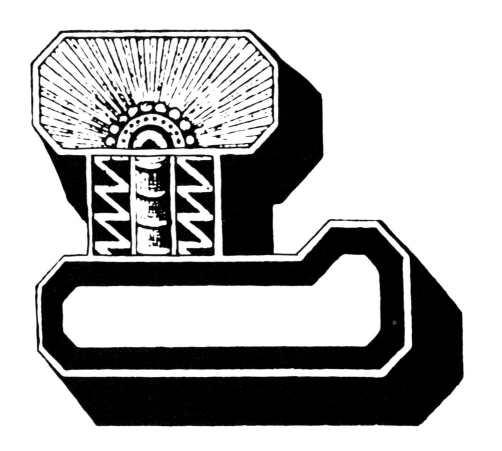

101

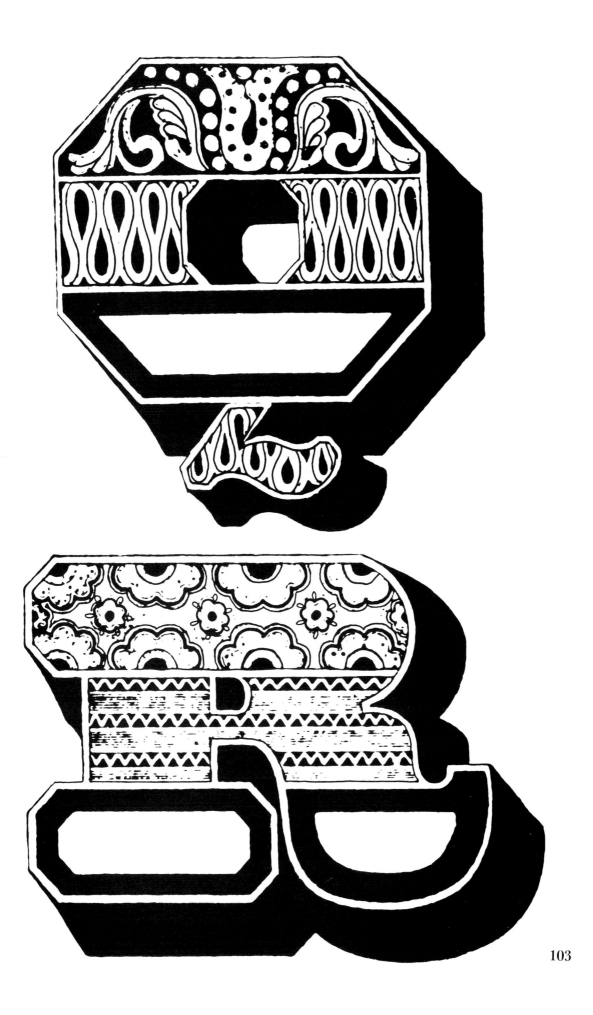

105

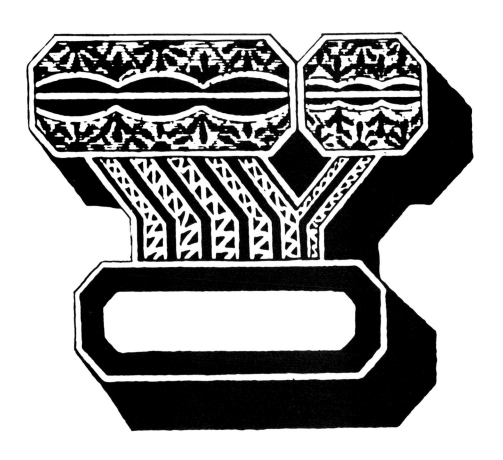

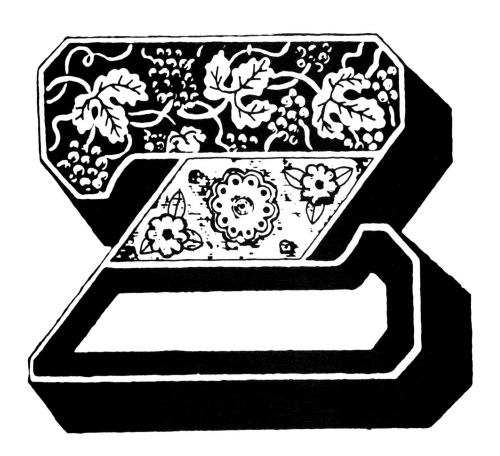

ABCD
EFGHIJ
KLMNOP
QRSTUV
WXYZ
123
456789

abcdefghijklm

nopqrstuvwxyz

&

ABCDEFGHIJK

LMNOPQRSTU

VWXYZ

ABCDEFGHIJ
KLMNOPQRS
TUVWXYZ

All of the letters in the alphabets are worked with 6-strand embroidery floss using the padded satin stitch. Pad the letter with outline, stem, or satin stitch. Cover them with satin stitches going horizontally across letters. When there is a curve in the letter, follow it around by adding a few more satin stitches on the wide outside of the curve creating a fan effect.

Pockets

Although embroidery and appliqué seem at first to be more decorative, pockets can be decorative as well as functional. There are many different kinds of pockets ranging from a simple patch to a pleated safari pocket with a flap, button, and buttonhole. One or several pockets can be applied to a garment, and can be embroidered, appliquéd, or topstitched before applying them to the garment, or can simply be hemmed. If you don't know what kind of pockets you would like to use, experiment. You can do this by drawing or tracing the basic garment and sketching different pockets on them, or by cutting the pockets out of paper and pinning them to the garment pieces to see if they work.

Once you have decided which pocket you want to use, make it in fabric, tracing the pattern directly from the book. Make any size changes on the paper pattern. Pockets can be made larger or smaller using the same graphing principles used for basic patterns. Add ½″ seam allowance on all pockets and flaps. If you are making a flat patch pocket, add 1½″ seam allowance at the top of the pocket for the hem, ½″ around the rest.

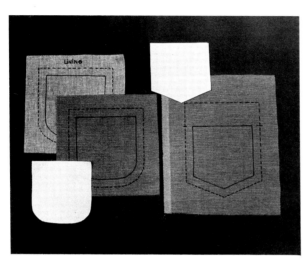

Add ½″ seam allowance on all pockets and flaps. For flat patch pockets, add 1½″ seam allowance at the top.

A pocket should be finished, except for the stitching that holds it to the garment, before it is applied. Any topstitching or decorative stitching should be done before the pocket is attached. If you wish to embroider or appliqué a pocket, cut the fabric large enough to fit in a hoop. Do the work, then cut the pocket to size allowing seams. I suggest lining for these pockets so that there are no loose threads on the inside.

Apply the pocket or pockets to the garment pieces before the entire garment is sewn together. If you are making a pair of pockets, make sure you line them up evenly. Place one pocket on the garment and then measure the distance from the center front and from the top or bottom of the garment to the pocket. Mark the corresponding measurements on the other side of the garment with pins, then place the second pocket. Sew the pockets on, tacking the top corners with a few stitches so they don't pull away when used.

The first few pocket patterns included here are simple, while the later ones are a little more difficult. However, once you master the few simple techniques, any pocket will seem easy. Some just take a bit more time to complete. In some cases you may be able to fit the pocket pattern pieces in between the pieces of the garment when it is laid on the fabric. If you are not sure you will have enough, buy extra fabric. If you plan to have buttons on flaps, buy extra buttons so they match any others you may be using.

GENERAL INFORMATION FOR POCKET PATTERNS

1. All of the patterns are printed without a seam allowance. Add ½″ all around each piece unless otherwise specified.

2. The dotted lines on the pattern pieces represent topstitching.

3. The straight grain on each pattern piece is marked with a double pointed arrow.

4. When there are 3 dots marked on a line (•⦂) place that line along the fold of the fabric on the straight grain.

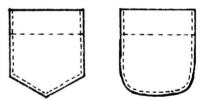

FLAT PATCH POCKETS

Flat patch pockets can be finished in two ways before they are applied to the garment. For straight edges, the seams can be turned back and pressed; for rounded edges, they can be lined, turned, pressed, and then applied.

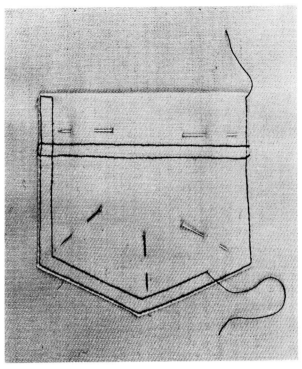

To hem, stitch ¼″, then fold the hem back and stitch 1¼″ and stitch side seams.

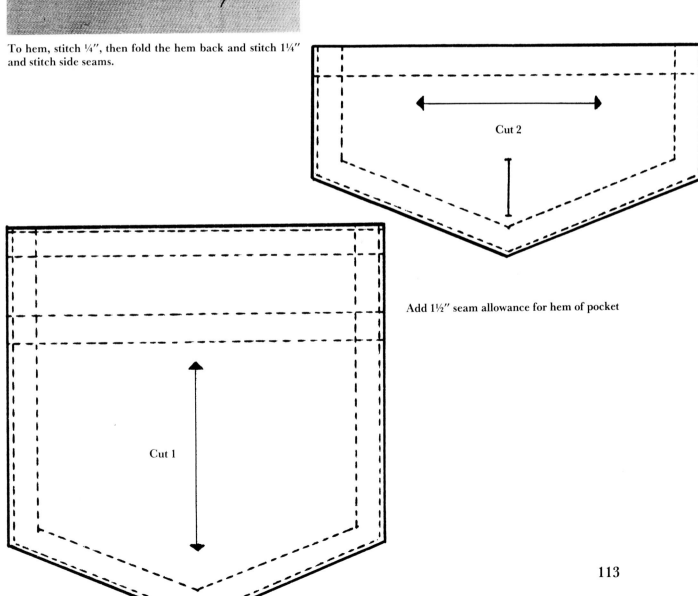

Cut 2

Add 1½″ seam allowance for hem of pocket

Cut 1

113

To finish the top of the pocket, turn the top edge back ¼″ and stitch. Then fold the hem back 1¼″ (right sides together), and stitch side seams closed. Turn the hem of the pocket right side out, press all the edges back ½″, and pin the pocket to

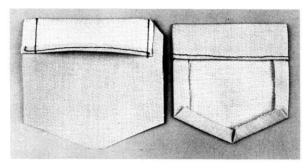

Topstitch the top edge of the pocket before applying it to the garment.

the garment. If you want to stitch down the hem of the pocket, do so before it is applied. When pinning the pocket to the garment, put the pins in at right angles to the pocket edges; basting is not necessary. Sew by machine, tacking the top edges of the pocket so they are sturdy.

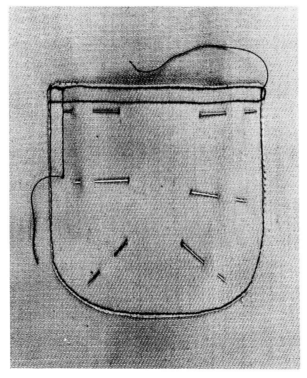

When pinning a pocket to the garment, put the pins in at right angles to the pocket edges.

If a patch pocket is an odd shape or has rounded edges, the pocket should be lined. Cut two identical pockets using ½″ seam allowance all around. One piece will be the front of the pocket and the other will be the lining. Linings can be cut out of the same fabric, if the fabric is not too heavy; otherwise use a lighter weight fabric. For accurate stitching, trace the shape of the finished pocket onto the lining and use this as a guide line for stitching. Place right sides of the pocket and lining together and seam around the whole pocket. Trim seam to ⅛″ and snip off the corners. Cut a slit about 2½″ long across the bottom of the lining, about ¾″ up. Pull the pocket through the slit, press flat, and sew the slit together with small slip stitches. Topstitch the top edge if you wish. Apply pocket to garment.

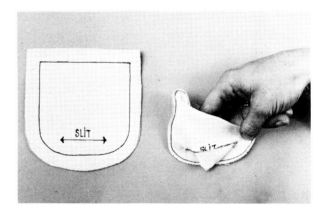

Cut a 2½″ slit in the lining of the pocket so the pocket can be turned.

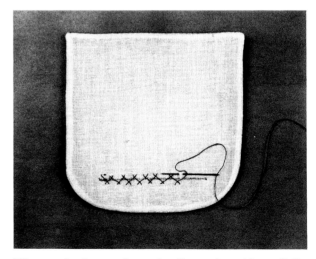

When pocket is turned, sew the slit together with small slip stitches.

114

ROUNDED PATCH POCKET
WITH OR WITHOUT FLAP

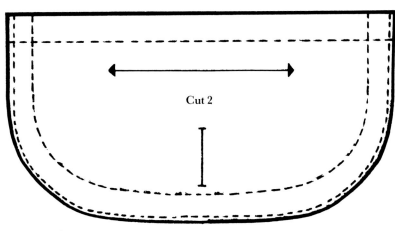

Cut 2

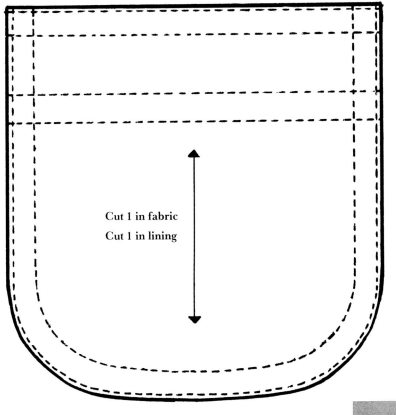

Cut 1 in fabric

Cut 1 in lining

PATCH POCKETS
WITH FLAPS

Make the basic flat patch pocket but do not stitch a wide hem at the top.

Flap: Cut out flap and lining including a ½″ seam allowance. (Flaps are always slightly wider than pocket so make sure they cover the edges.) Place

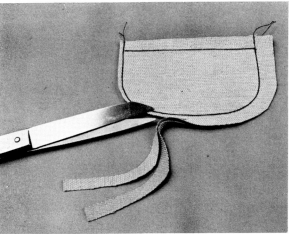

Trim seam of pocket and lining to ⅛″ before turning pocket.

right sides of flap and lining together, and seam leaving top open for turning. Trim seams, turn, press, and topstitch the edges if you wish. If you want a buttonhole on the flap, put it on now. Apply the pocket itself, measure up ½″ from the top of the pocket, and place flap along this line, with the right sides of flap and garment together.

Stitch a ⅛″ seam along flap edge. Turn flap down, press, and stitch across, ¼″ to ½″ down from the top of the flap. Make sure this stitched seam covers the raw seam underneath. Sew a button on the pocket in its proper place. Make sure you don't sew the pocket closed when stitching on the button.

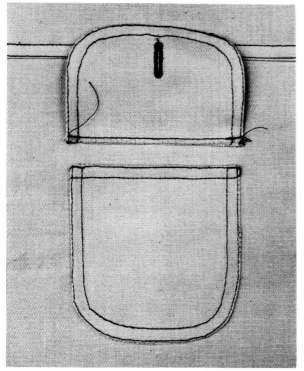

To apply a flap, measure up ½″ from the pocket, and stitch flap to this line, right sides together.

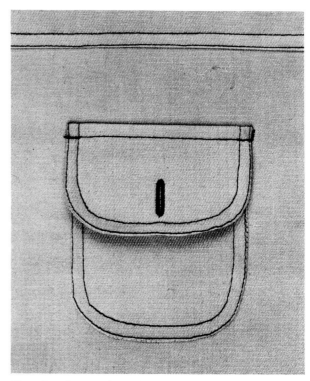

Turn flap down and topstitch across, ¼″ to ½″ from the top of the flap.

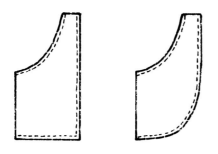

JEAN POCKETS

Jean pockets should be lined completely if they are going on a dress, smock, or jacket. Follow the lining instructions for "Patch Pockets," page 114.

If they are going on pants or shorts, the top and sides of the pocket can be left raw because they will be sewn in the seams of the garment.

If the pockets are not lined, finish off the pocket opening with double fold ½″ bias tape. Open the tape, place right side of tape to right side of pocket and stitch along fold of tape. Trim seams, clip curves, turn bias back, and press. Topstitch on right side to hold tape in place.

If you are making the straight edge pocket, simply turn the edge back and press a ½″ seam allowance. Pin pocket to garment, line up top and side of the pocket with top and side seam of pants, and stitch.

116

On rounded jean pockets, stitch bias tape right sides to-gether to the rounded edges of the pocket.

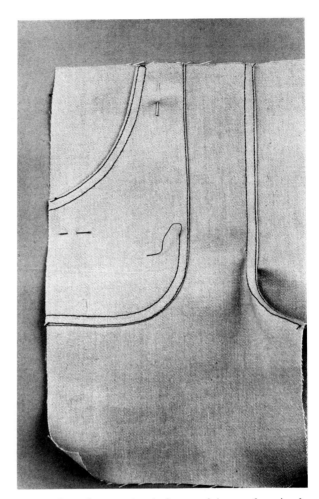

Topstitch pocket opening before applying pocket. Apply topstitching to the rest of the pocket as you stitch on the pocket itself. Note that side edge of pocket is included with the seam of the garment.

For the rounded edge jean pocket, finish both curved edges with bias tape and turn bias back. On pocket opening, topstitch to hold tape in place, leave other curve only pressed. Pin to garment and stitch.

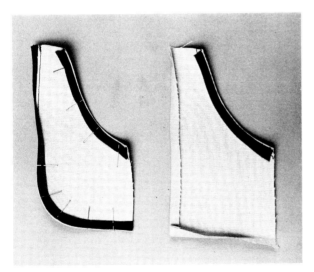

Bias tape on jean pockets: Rounded pocket needs bias tape on all rounded edges; straight-edged pocket requires bias tape only at pocket opening.

117

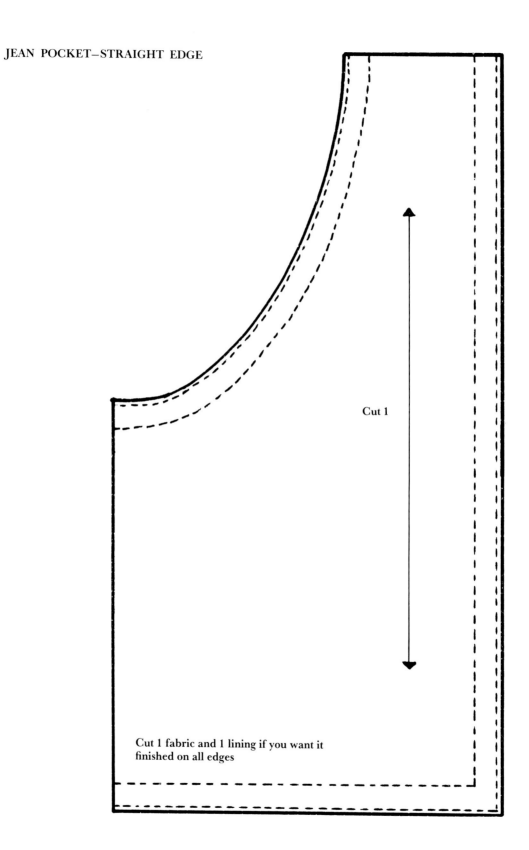

Cut 1

Cut 1 fabric and 1 lining if you want it
finished on all edges

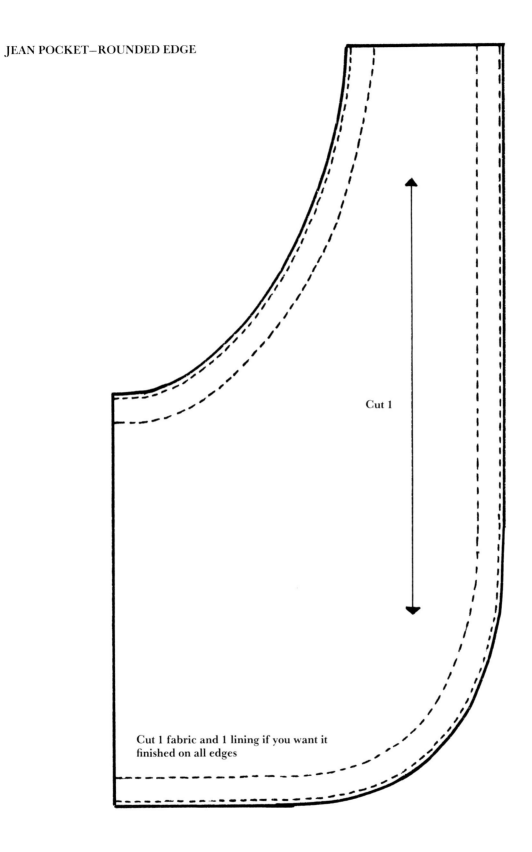

Cut 1

Cut 1 fabric and 1 lining if you want it
finished on all edges

POUCH POCKETS

Cut pocket and lining with ½″ seam allowance all around. Seam pocket and lining all around, placing right sides together. Trim seams, slit, turn, sew slit closed, and press pocket flat. Top-stitch any open edges, if you wish. Place pocket on garment and stitch. To separate the pouch into small pockets, draw dividing lines and stitch through both the pocket and the garment.

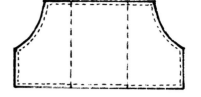

POUCH POCKET JEAN STYLE

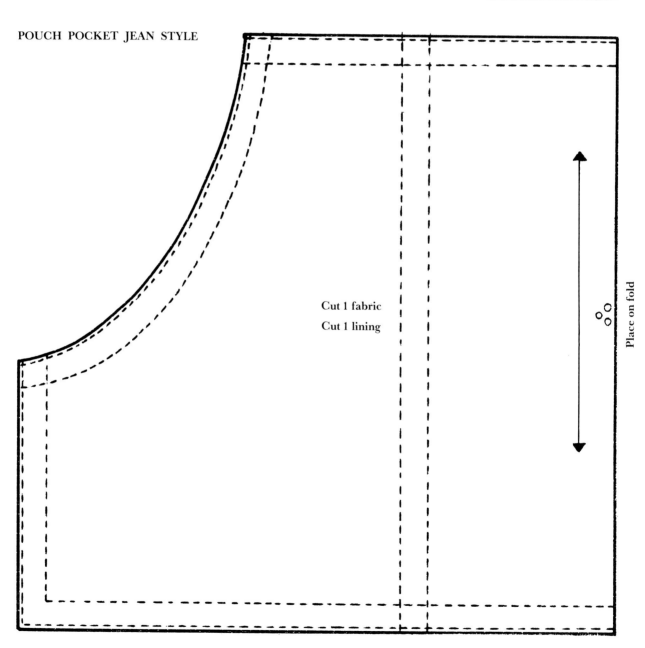

Cut 1 fabric

Cut 1 lining

Place on fold

120

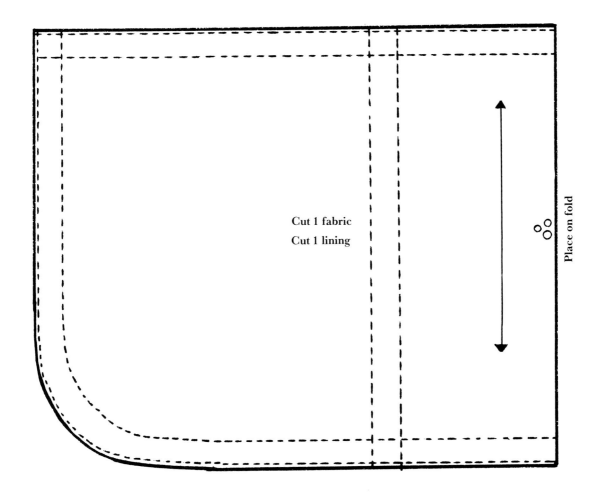

Cut 1 fabric
Cut 1 lining

Place on fold

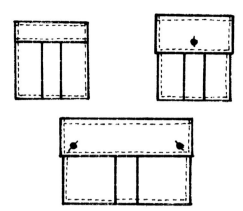

SAFARI POCKETS

Cut pockets and flaps with ½″ seam allowance. Snip notches on each side and in the center of the pleat on the pocket. Sew the pleat together by folding pocket in half with wrong sides together and seaming along pleat line. Open the pleat, match notch to center seam, and press flat. Turn back ½″ and stitch top of pocket.

If the pocket is to have a top band, place one side of band on top of the pocket right sides together, matching notches, and stitch across. Press seam allowances up toward the top. Fold band right sides together, and stitch sides down. Turn, press edges back ½″ all around, and topstitch band, if you wish. Apply the pocket to garment.

For the flapped safari pocket, finish the pocket and apply it to the garment. Then finish the flap in the same manner as patch pocket flap.

To add top band, stitch band to pocket, right sides together. Press seam allowance toward the top, fold band back, and stitch sides.

After side seams have been made, turn the band right side out.

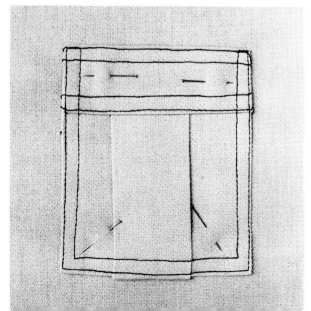

Topstitch the band, if you wish. Then stitch the pocket to the garment.

To make safari pocket pleat, fold pocket in half, wrong sides together, stitch along pleat line, match notch to center seam, and press flat.

SAFARI POCKET WITH TOP BAND

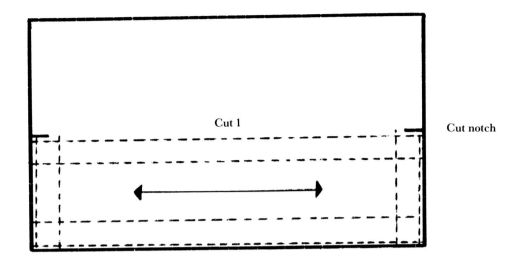

Cut 1

Cut notch

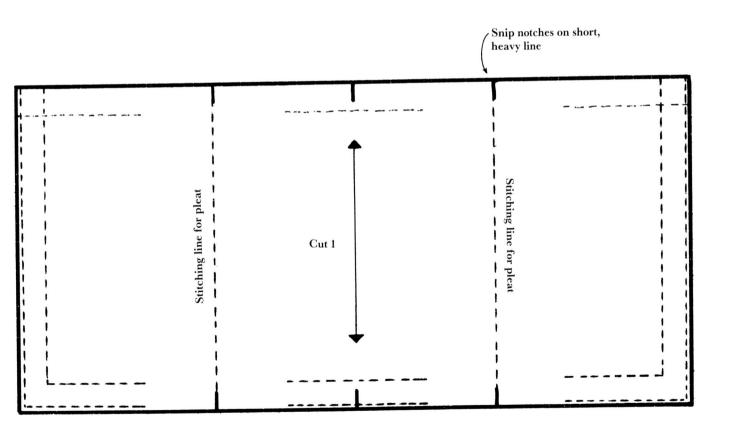

Snip notches on short, heavy line

Stitching line for pleat

Stitching line for pleat

Cut 1

SAFARI POUCH POCKET
WITH BUTTON FLAP

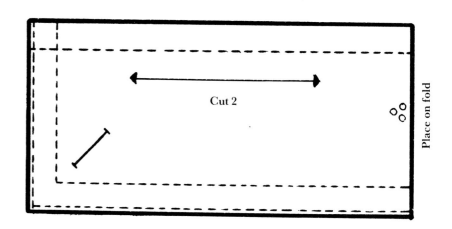

Cut 2

Place on fold

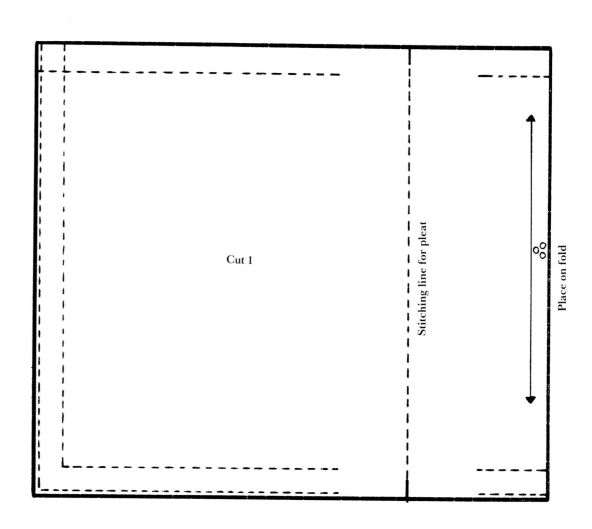

Cut 1

Stitching line for pleat

Place on fold

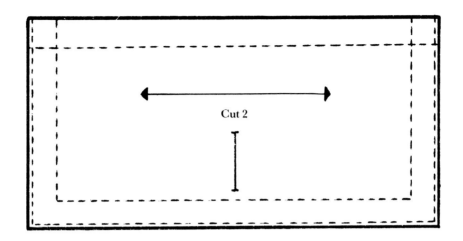

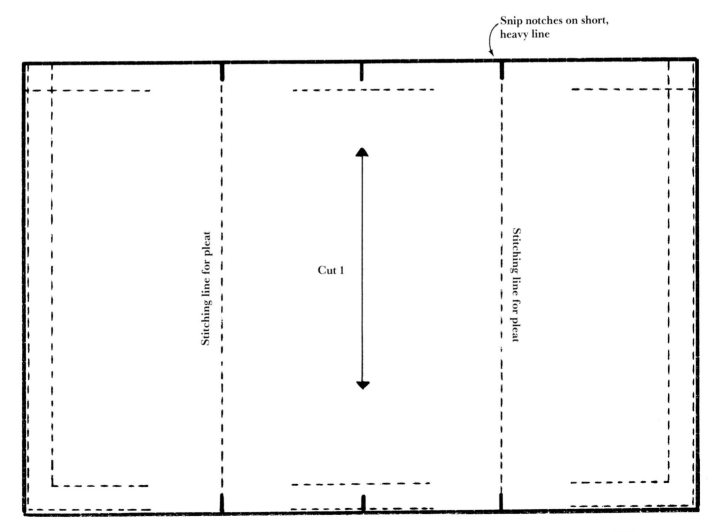

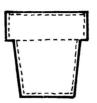

FLOWER POT POCKET

Appliqué or embroider a flower or tree to garment before you apply the pocket, so the flower or tree appears to be growing from the pocket. Cut out the pot pocket and lining with ½″ seam allowance. Seam pocket and lining together, trim seams, slit, turn, and press. Topstitch pocket if you wish, then apply to garment.

FLOWER POT POCKET

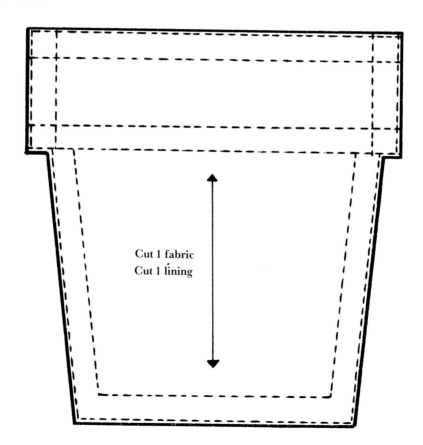

Cut 1 fabric
Cut 1 lining

126

PATCH BLOCK POCKET

Cut out each piece of the block with ¼″ seam allowance. Each section of the block can be a different patterned fabric or a different color. Cut out 1 piece for the lining in the shape of the entire block. Join the pieces of the block together and press. Place right sides of pocket and lining together and stitch all around. Trim seams, slit, turn, and press. Apply pocket to garment by machine or with small hemming stitches used to appliqué.

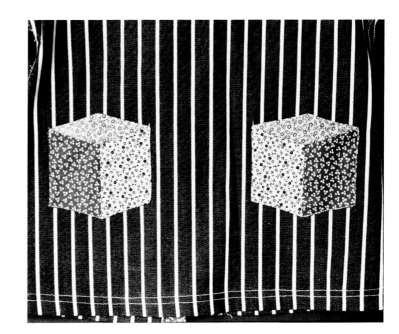

PATCH BLOCK POCKET

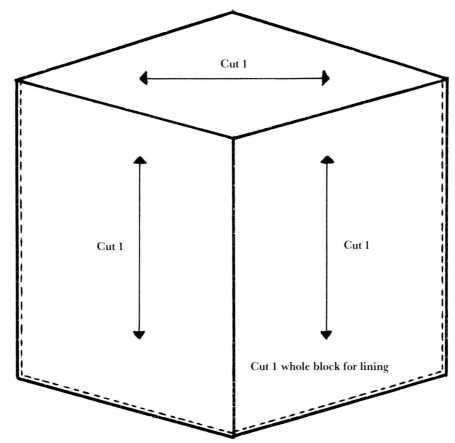

Cut 1

Cut 1

Cut 1

Cut 1 whole block for lining

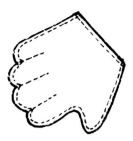

TRACED HAND POCKETS

To make a pattern for this pocket you can either trace the child's hand or take the pattern from the book. If you trace the hand, round the fingers at the edges so they can be turned easily. Cut a pocket and a lining with ½″ seam allowance. Place rights sides together, seam, slit, trim seams, turn, and press. Apply to the garment by machine or use the hemming stitch used for appliqué.

TRACED HAND POCKET

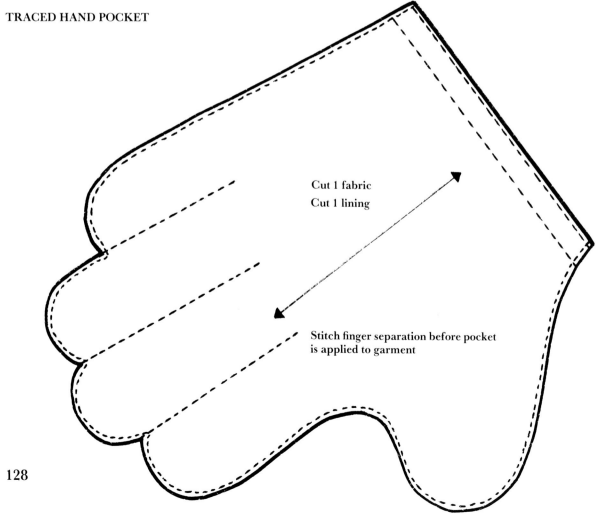

Cut 1 fabric
Cut 1 lining

Stitch finger separation before pocket is applied to garment